LEMONS

LEMONS to Lemonade

Resolving Problems in Meetings, Workshops, and PLCs

Robert J.
Garmston
●●●●●●●●●●●●
Diane P.
Zimmerman

CORWIN
A SAGE Company

CORWIN
A SAGE Company

FOR INFORMATION:

Corwin

A SAGE Company

2455 Teller Road

Thousand Oaks, California 91320

(800) 233-9936

www.corwin.com

SAGE Publications Ltd.

1 Oliver's Yard

55 City Road

London EC1Y 1SP

United Kingdom

SAGE Publications India Pvt. Ltd.

B 1/I 1 Mohan Cooperative Industrial Area

Mathura Road, New Delhi 110 044

India

SAGE Publications Asia-Pacific Pte. Ltd.

3 Church Street

#10-04 Samsung Hub

Singapore 049483

Printed in the United States of America

A catalog record of this book is available from the Library of Congress.

ISBN 978-1-4522-6101-0

This book is printed on acid-free paper.

Acquisitions Editor: Arnis Burvikovs

Associate Editor: Desirée A. Bartlett

Editorial Assistant: Mayan White

Project Editor: Amy Schroller

Copy Editor: Codi Bowman

Typesetter: C&M Digitals (P) Ltd.

Proofreader: Theresa Kay

Indexer: Sylvia Coates

Cover Designer: Candice Harman

Permissions Editor: Jennifer Barron

SUSTAINABLE FORESTRY INITIATIVE
Label applies to the text stock

Certified Sourcing
www.sfiprogram.org
SFI-00341

13 14 15 16 17 10 9 8 7 6 5 4 3 2 1

CONTENTS

LIST OF FIGURES AND ILLUSTRATIONS

PUBLISHER'S ACKNOWLEDGMENTS

Corwin gratefully acknowledges the contributions of the following reviewers:

Dr. Patricia Conner
District Test Coordinator
Berryville Public Schools
Berryville, AR

Dr. John F. Eller
Author, Professor
St. Cloud State University
St. Cloud, MN

Sheila A. Eller
Author, Principal
Bel Air Elementary
New Brighton, MN

Robbi Schranz
Literacy Coach
Waupun Area School District
Waupun, WI

ABOUT THE AUTHORS

ROBERT J. GARMSTON, EdD, is an Emeritus Professor of Educational Administration at California State University, Sacramento, and Founder of Facilitation Associates located in Sacramento, California, and Cofounder of The Center for Cognitive Coaching and the Center for Adaptive Schools (www.thinking collaborative), both located in Denver, Colorado. Formerly a classroom teacher, principal, director of instruction, and acting superintendent, he works as an educational consultant specializing in leadership, learning, and personal and organizational development. He has made presentations and conducted workshops for teachers, administrators, and staff developers throughout the United States as well as in Canada, Africa, Asia, Australia, Europe, and the Middle East.

Bob has practiced meeting management in each of his leadership roles, and for thirty years, he has taught facilitation skills, presentation skills, and group management to educational leaders. He taught meeting management in Copenhagen to supervisors in the World Health Organization. He studied under Michael Doyle and David Strauss, cofounders of the Interaction Method of Conducting Meetings. In the 1980s, he formed a group in Northern California to study and refine facilitation techniques. For four years, he wrote a column on managing meetings from the perspectives of presenters and facilitators for the *Journal of Staff Development,* a publication of the National Staff Development Council, now Learning Forward.

Bob has written and coauthored a number of books including *Cognitive Coaching: A Foundation for Renaissance Schools, How to Make Presentations That Teach and Transform, The Adaptive School: A Sourcebook for Collaborative Groups, A Presenter's Fieldbook: A Practical Guide, Unlocking Group Potential for School Improvement,* and a memoir, *I Don't Do That Anymore: A Memoir of Awakening and Resilience.* He has been recognized by NSDC for his contributions to staff development. His work has been translated into Arabic, Hebrew, Italian, and Spanish.

In addition to educational clients, he has worked with diverse groups including police officers, probation officers, court and justice systems, utilities districts, the United States Air Force, and the World Health Organization.

DIANE P. ZIMMERMAN, PhD, is a writer and consultant focusing on entrepreneurial learning and schools that make a difference. She obtained her PhD in Human and Organizational Development from the Fielding Graduate Institute. She recently retired as a superintendent of schools after a 36-year career in education that was rich in leadership, facilitation, and conflict management.

Trained originally as a speech therapist, Diane worked early in her career as a teacher, speech therapist, program manager, and assistant director of special education in Fairfield, California. She subsequently became a principal in Davis, California, and served consecutively in two schools more than 13 years before being promoted to assistant superintendent for personnel. In 2002, she began a nine-year journey as a superintendent of Old Adobe School Union School District, a small suburban elementary school district in Petaluma, California. She prides herself in moving the district's teachers from contentious union interactions to cooperative collaborations as productive, interest-based educators who collectively set the highest standards possible for their school district.

Diane has been active in professional development all of her career. While obtaining her administrative credential, Diane was assigned to Bob Garmston as her intern coach. This early career interaction turned in to a lifelong intellectual partnership, and Diane became an influential leader in the Cognitive Coaching consulting consortium founded by Bob Garmston and Art Costa.

Diane has taught in administrative training programs at several northern California universities, and over the past 20 years she has written and consulted in the areas of Cognitive Coaching, teacher supervision and evaluation, facilitation, stages of adult development, assessment of leadership skills, and constructivist leadership.

Leadership and mediation of conflict has always been a part of Diane's life. She was encouraged to assume leadership roles throughout her career, from early work supervising in a family restaurant business, to her first teaching job in a new special education program, through her years as a principal. Throughout her career, she has been involved in handling divergent opinions and mediating conflict. She gained a substantive reputation as the in-house expert in facilitation, and her staff valued her ability to create learning communities long before professional learning communities were popularized.

INTRODUCTION

T he purpose of this book is to extend the reader's practical knowledge of successful ways to anticipate and correct the many events that can go wrong in professional gatherings—meetings, professional development sessions, PLC deliberations, and the like. Teacher leaders, mentors, site administrators, curriculum coordinators, staff developers, and district administrators will find the ideas here useful. While written with educators in mind, the principles and ideas are fully applicable in business, community organizations, and the military. We have worked in each of these sectors.

Leaders of work groups and presenters will find the tools in this book useful to help them manage learning environments, and those who lead meetings in which the purpose is to plan, explore ideas, assess programs, or make decisions will use these ideas consistently. While our focus is on disruptive events—what goes wrong in sessions—our mission is to create teamwork that fosters success—to create lemonade. To be specific, success means getting work done efficiently, honestly, and with great integrity.

As our work world becomes more complex, social networks denser, and the need for collaboration greater, meetings have become commonplace. Anytime more than three people come together to get something done we think of it as a meeting, and we believe that this collaborative work deserves purposeful attention. We advocate that all participants share a responsibility for the effectiveness of these gatherings. Successful meetings do not happen by accident. There are three common complaints about meetings: (1) They waste our time, (2) we never get to real issues either because participants often do not speak up or one person dominates, and (3) disagreements and conflict render the sessions not only unproductive but unsafe. This book is a practical tool kit for the facilitator who wishes to address these issues, and more than this, any member of a group can make a difference by practicing skills in this book. Our vision of effective meetings is that everyone is a facilitator. In fact, many of the communication strategies are effective across all the human domains of interaction in which we could benefit by being open, honest, and tactful. We believe that responsibility for successful meetings should be part of the expected work ethic—meetings are serious business and everyone is responsible for making them effective. The techniques outlined in this book are organized from novice to expert, providing interventions for all kinds of meeting snafus. While this is essentially a how-to book, we want to stress the importance of personal wisdom—your own experiences and reflections. We will use the term *facilitator* to describe the function of managing a meeting, no matter what name you might give to this role in your organization. Over time, accomplished facilitators learn just when to intervene with counterproductive participants and events and develop finely tuned intervention radar to know how to turn problems into learning opportunities. Like turning lemons into lemonade, the accomplished facilitator takes what is and improvises to create what existed before only in the realm of possible.

TO INTERCEDE IS TO LEAD

To intervene means to take action to change what is happening or might happen to prevent counterproductive behaviors and increase group productivity and learning. When we intercede, we intervene on behalf of another—in this case on behalf of the group. The facilitator must always ask, "Is this intervention in the best interest of the group?" However, we are also interceding on behalf of individuals in that our interventions need to tactfully guide and direct unproductive behavior to more productive channels. When this is done skillfully, all save face and feel safe. For example, when a group member begins to dominate the meeting, a facilitator might give the direction, "Turn to your neighbor and talk about what other ideas would be important for the group to consider. Be prepared to share." Or a facilitator might say, "Let's hear from someone who hasn't talked yet," and wait until other hands go up. Or a facilitator might say, "I notice that one person is doing most of the talking. Earlier you agreed to balance participation. Take a moment and talk with your neighbor about why you think this is happening. Be prepared to share."

This book encourages readers to participate vicariously. For each intervention strategy we included, we asked ourselves, "Have we done this?" or "Would we perform this particular intervention?" Readers are invited to stand on our shoulders and on the shoulders of those we have learned from to accelerate their successes and, we hope, shorten the trial-and-error part of the learning sequence. There are no right answers in facilitation but only approaches to challenges, and so there can be no guarantees; however, this book offers multiple solutions to help facilitators increase their intervention repertoires and chances for success.

We intend to serve both those who are seeking to improve their facilitation skills and those skilled facilitators who want to extend their knowledge base about intervening when things go wrong. Probably no single facilitator has used all of the intervention strategies described in this book, so at whatever level the reader is, we anticipate there will opportunities to add to one's repertoire.

WHY READ THIS BOOK

"Meetings are as common as dirt and about as popular."

(Weisbord & Janoff, 2007, p. ix)

A major source of the low status of meetings, and sometimes other public gatherings like in-service sessions, comes from disruptions that are not effectively addressed. George Kieffer (1988), in his book *The Strategy of Meetings,* says that meetings are essentially mobs in waiting. They are easily susceptible to passions and manipulations. Time is wasted, goodwill is lost, and environments that should be productive sometimes become unsafe. This book is about managing those unexpected occurrences that crop up when groups of people work together, and using these events to build group cohesion, productivity, and learning. The facilitator's most important job is to develop the group's resources while learning the craft of facilitating and adding intervention strategies. Interventions take on added power when facilitators learn to use strategies in ways to help groups work smarter. In short, this book is about how powerful interventions from a skilled leader can cement a group's commitment to improved work that produces better results.

Groups are harder to manage than individuals. Many minds mean many perspectives, and in the worst of cases, groups will exhibit dysfunctional tendencies like the law of triviality and avoidance, spending maximum time on matters of least importance—putting disproportionate weight on trivial issues. Ironically, when topics are safe, everyone has an opinion and groups tend to speak up, becoming verbose. However, when a nontrivial issue comes up, the group may become silent. So simply forming a group does not mean that members are skilled in functioning together. Groups are complex, nuanced entities requiring skilled leadership and collective knowledge of how best to work. From PLCs, to departments, to staff meetings, to advisory groups, forming a group is but a first step toward collective goals. Often in these settings problems arise from well intentioned but unskilled people. *From Lemons to Lemonade* will aid in resurrecting the positive energy and goodwill that should pervade group settings. Readers will be able to anticipate and prevent problems before they occur and gain confidence in addressing those that still sneak in the door. Time will be used more effectively. Greater senses of positivity will prevail. Groups will gain faith in their power to make a difference in their work.

Like *Unlocking Group Potential to Improve Schools* (Garmston with von Frank, 2012), this is a field guide inspired by more than 40 years of working with groups. While working on *Unlocking Group Potential,* Bob talked with leaders about common problems they encountered with groups. Out of that and our own experiences grew the exhaustive list of issues contained in this book.

In addition, accomplished facilitators learn that while they are in charge of process, they also are serving the group—and must trust the group's wisdom about itself. When any of the strategies in this book are used primarily to control a decision or to drive content in a particular direction, groups will sense the difference and distrust the process and the facilitator. Accomplished facilitators are sensitive to their personal beliefs as well as the group's needs. Chapter 2 describes how to take care of yourself first and then take care of others.

The book is organized into three introductory chapters and four how-to chapters.

To build a repertoire of interventions, read cover-to-cover. Some readers, however, may want to go directly to one section to learn a few intervention strategies, and so the problem locator in Figure I.1 may help to identify chapters relevant to specific situations.

Time, experience, strategies, mental rehearsal, and reflection contribute to the facilitator's ability to develop critical premises about intervening. A skilled facilitator knows the relationship is with the group, not the individual. That understanding helps those leading groups to have the backbone to assertively intervene without sacrificing the group to keep one member happy.

As you take time to understand and learn more about the art of direct intervention, you will be able to see how treating each group member with dignity and respect enables interventions to succeed. The latter four chapters are organized for increasingly direct interventions that may, in some cases, even be uncomfortably assertive.

The learning of all complex behaviors requires time, patience, practice, and reflection. Stay the journey—and celebrate each success.

Figure I.1 Problem Locater

Challenges	Location	Strategies
Facilitator is attacked	Chapters 1 and 7	The six-step response
Insufficient confidence	Chapters 1 and 2	Mental rehearsal, centering, identity as a facilitator, room arrangement, and evaluating self and group on a proficiency scale
Managing personal emotions	Chapter 2	Overcoming discomfort, nervousness, becoming centered, staying true to who you are in response to stressors and circle of excellence
Overcoming judgmental responses	Chapter 2	Presume positive intentions
Creating an adequate environment	Chapter 2 and Appendix	Address environmental details that distract group members: room arrangement, seating, temperature, and noise pollution
Intervening with consistency, clarity, and safety	Chapter 3	Respond with compassion, use precise language, and determine risk levels
Deciding when and how to intervene	Chapter 4	Assure standards and working agreements, evaluate working agreements, recalibrate, clarify tasks, manage group energies and emotions, and keep work relevant

(Continued)

Figure I.1 (Continued)

Challenges	Location	Strategies
Getting attention and focus, managing workflow breakdowns, emotional outbursts, and power struggles	Chapter 5	Attention first, signals, proximity, refocusing moves, redirecting engagement, energizing a quiet group, and managing emotions from positions to interests
Managing low engagement and problem behaviors	Chapter 6	Ignoring the knitter, intervening with the nonparticipant, daydreamer, silent person, frowner, and distracted participant
Managing disruptive participants	Chapter 6	Interventions for the broken record, long-winded speaker, humorist, inappropriate humorist, late comer, early leaver, resister, side talker, know-it-all, monopolizer, rhetorician, overly articulate, pedagogical isolate, misinformant, interrupter, subject changer, and texter
Managing complex situations	Chapter 7	
Group conflict		Grounding and existing-desired state
Demoralizing external events		Desired state, third point, redirecting resistance, pace and lead, and structured interviews
Disputes		Verbalize the issue, acknowledge each position, identify source of information, check perceptions, and reframe conflict as asset

Challenges	Location	Strategies
Dissenting views		Paraphrasing partner, pace the emotion, redirect attacks, reframe the opposition, use styles, assumptions wall, brainstorm questions, and disperse to agree
Personal attacks		The six-step response, step between opposing members, change the narrative, and enlist the group in solving the problem
Challenges to the leader		Process commercial, engage with more intensity, engage with less intensity, and request civility
Subgroup manipulation		Decision matrix, values decision matrix, require a quorum, pace-lead-poll, one-minute advocacy, and alternate microphone advocacy
Sabotage		Surface tensions, cynic as frustrated optimist, pair up and explore sabotage, and elephant walk
Irresolvable conflicts		Polarity management

1

THE NOVICE TO EXPERT JOURNEY

I n this chapter, we describe how facilitators can move from novice to expert levels in their ability to intervene when disruptive events occur. Readers will be able to place themselves along a continuum of novice to expert and learn about appropriate next steps at their stage of the journey. We begin with an example that demonstrates the work of an expert facilitator—knowing just how and when to intervene to keep both individuals and group members working toward productive ends.

The group is challenging. Participants' resistance is growing, and suddenly, a strident voice bursts out, "This is a waste of time!" Group members hold their breaths and wait for the facilitator's next move. The facilitator's response to this kind of challenge separates the novice from the expert. A novice may try to justify and run the risk of getting into an argument. The expert knows how to listen and move toward a resolution.

Consider this expert series of moves demonstrated by a colleague. As he tells it, 90 minutes into a work session, a teacher angrily shouted out, "What does this have to do with algebra?" Even an experienced facilitator will be taken aback by unexpected

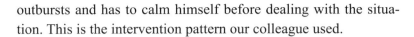

outbursts and has to calm himself before dealing with the situation. This is the intervention pattern our colleague used.

Step 1: Paused, breathed, and moved toward the speaker. This is an important step because it helps the facilitator monitor and adjust his internal state.

Step 2: Asked for the speaker's name. From this point on, the conversation is no longer anonymous.

Step 3: Used the speaker's tone to paraphrase so that the speaker knew that his emotion was understood. In a firm, but slightly angry tone, the facilitator said something like, "You're upset because what we are doing seems like a waste of time to you." Getting agreement about the speaker's emotional state is a critical move. The speaker responds with an affirmation or a clarification.

Step 4: The facilitator made a polite inquiry as to the difficulty the speaker was having and began to move the conversation toward productive resolution. Now in a normal tone of voice he said, "Help me understand the problem you are having." He attempted to talk through the difficulty. This step does not take more than a minute of group time. If a resolution will take longer, the facilitator moves to the next step.

Step 5: The facilitator in this case said something like, "I now recognize that this challenge deserves more time than we have right now. Can you hang out until the break when we can work to resolve the issue?"

Step 6: At break time, the facilitator had a private conversation in an attempt to resolve the issue. Most people will agree to meet at the break, and 99% of the time, they will show up ready to solve the problem. They often just want to be listened to, and once they are, their resistance evaporates. For those not willing to meet at the break, the expert facilitator moves to Step 7.

Step 7: The facilitator would say, "You seem to be between a rock and a hard place. On the one hand, you feel mandated to be here; on the other hand, you are not producing value for yourself and your students. You have a difficult choice. Stay here and I will do what I can to help you make connections to your students, or leave the room and do something else that will benefit your algebra students more than being here. Know that I will support you 100% whichever decision you make." With that, the facilitator would turn and walk away from the participant, enforcing the principle of never taking choice away in difficult confrontations.

This example demonstrates the work of an expert facilitator—knowing just how and when to intervene to keep both individuals and group members working toward productive ends. The point is the facilitator was able to recognize this outburst as threatening to the group, was able to ground himself, and worked directly with the situation. With his actions, he communicated in a way that the group learned that such outbursts would be handled safely and respectfully. He demonstrated his clear intention to protect the group and his commitment to a larger theme—that the time spent together should be useful. He communicated a deep respect for group members' right to dissent while also requiring the dissenter to become part of the solution.

A facilitator without much experience will have a much more difficult time when faced with threatening challenges. Beginners faced with such animosity often crumble as their brain, specifically the amygdala, goes into overdrive and urges the body toward automatic responses appropriate to physical danger, wiping from their motor memory the rules they might have learned for dealing with disruptions. Novice facilitators necessarily relegate the majority of their attention trying to practice rudimentary facilitation techniques, or they become distracted or flustered when things do not go according to plan. Much of the time, the novice responds with a defensive posture or judgmentally.

Accomplished facilitators respond elegantly to the unexpected because they've learned how to effectively anticipate, predict, and modify their approaches to problems in the moment as necessary. Expert facilitators' learning arc is enhanced because they are self-directed learners—self-monitoring, self-reflective, and self-modifying. Over time, they have rehearsed and practiced sequences of moves, and they are able to link complex moves together into coherent and successful interventions.

To intervene means to take action to change what is happening or might happen to prevent counterproductive behaviors. The goals for intervening always are to improve group performance or to develop the group's capacity for effective and efficient work. We believe that effective intervention is a moral imperative; time is a valuable asset that ought not to be wasted, and when all voices contribute, the sum is greater than the parts.

WE ALL BEGIN AS NOVICES

A novice is someone who has not yet acquired the skills and experience needed to perform a trade, a career, or a profession—in this case, the skills of intervention. To a novice, the expert's skills may seem invisible or even magical. They are unaware of the expert's subtle abilities to recognize patterns and possibilities. Based on these, the expert is also clear about intentions and follows through on these intentions in congruent ways.

In medicine, doctors serve internships. In business, beginning executives often are mentored. As they are mentored, beginners are expected to hone their metacognitive skills, along with increasing their knowledge and performance-related skills, to speed the journey to becoming an accomplished professional. In the teaching profession, novices are called "beginning teachers" and provided special support during their novice years. Beginning facilitators seldom have such deliberate support. Often, novice facilitators have limited practice time. The information in this book gives leaders a head start with skills we have honed over the course of two careers. We offer you an opportunity to envision success by learning from our experiences as experts in the field. The journey to competence takes time, commitment, and patience.

Everyone starts as a novice and, over time, in the right settings with much practice, can become accomplished in successfully intervening with groups. Working toward a status of expert or accomplished facilitator must be a conscious decision. Remembering our years as novices, we recognize that becoming an expert facilitator is a journey that never ends. Just when we think we have mastered the art, a group challenges us in ways that require new expertise, and we are once again improvising new solutions.

Authors Malcolm Gladwell (2008) and Matthew Syed (2010) point out that in any field, expertise is less a matter of talent than of practice. The term *expert* has come to mean a person with an unassailable grasp of the field, one who operates at not merely a good level, but at a level nearer to perfect. Several studies have shown that people enter this rarified state after many hours of engagement and practice—10,000 hours is the figure most commonly used.

Because investing thousands of hours in refining facilitation skills is not feasible for most, we use the term *accomplished* to represent the end of the continuum toward which we strive. Gladwell (2008) and Syed (2010) emphasize that novices need to work through trial and error and to become responsible for figuring out solutions. A coach or mentor may help along the way, but in the end, the learner is in control of the skills that are practiced and that become part of an ever-increasing repertoire.

ACCOMPLISHED MEANS COMPETENT

The path to mastery requires that learners move through five phases—from being unaware or uninformed to becoming highly accomplished and able to use skills both consciously and unconsciously. The keys to mastery are time and persistence. Figure 1.1 shows the path from being uniformed to accomplished facilitation.

Uninformed

At this stage, the facilitator is simply unaware of responsibilities and strategies associated with intervening. Facilitators view meetings as necessary and outside of their overt control.

Novice

The true novice level is *conscious incompetence*—knowing what one doesn't know. The novice realizes there is a better way. In

Figure 1.1 The Learner's Path—From Uninformed to Highly Accomplished

Uninformed *Unconscious incompetence*	The individual is not aware of what he or she doesn't know.
Novice *Conscious incompetence*	The facilitator knows that more elegant ways to respond exist, but needs to learn control and to acquire mental maps and intervention strategies. She needs opportunities to practice, both in real time and through mental rehearsal. Trial and error is necessary to learning.
Proficient *Conscious competence*	The facilitator is not fluent or elegant in the face of uncertainty, but is able to respond and adapt. He needs to consciously focus, meaning responses are purposeful and require mental energy that will not be needed as more expertise develops. The facilitator is just beginning to improvise and adapt. He requires mental energy and may lapse into decision fatigue.
Accomplished *Unconscious competence*	The facilitator is accomplished and able to respond, adapt, and improvise in the face of uncertainty. She has committed many complex moves to routine memory and no longer requires conscious thought to access these skills. The facilitator trusts herself and maintains control, even when faced with the unexpected.
Highly accomplished/ expert *Conscious of unconscious competence*	The facilitator recognizes all the levels of learning and can explicate and consciously model the nuances of the discipline. He recognizes the need for learners to go through these phases and that interventions and strategies may be different for each phase. This is the optimum level to be a teacher of others.

this valuable phase of learning, the learner begins to identify and focus on appropriate learning goals and to practice skills. This practitioner sets goals but does not have the knowledge, skills, and experience to be fluent. Many people cycle between *conscious incompetence* and *conscious competence*—just when one skill is mastered, a group offers a new challenge that makes the facilitator aware once more of her incompetence. Moving out of this stage requires persistence. Taking time after the public performance to mentally rehearse other strategies is helpful. (See box.)

Mental Rehearsal Improves Performance

Researchers are finding that mental rehearsal can be as valuable as actual practice (McTaggart, 2008). In mental imagery, athletes imagine they are actually competing, breaking down the game into tiny components and visualizing how they might improve specific aspects. Both EMG and electroencephalogram tests have shown that the brain does not differentiate between a thought and an action (Iacaboni, 2008). In tests with skiers, basketball players, weightlifters, boxers, and even those dealing with illness, the brain's electrical activity is the same whether the individual is thinking about doing something or actually doing it. We believe that facilitators can learn to mentally rehearse scenarios with difficult groups and to edit these scenes to imagine themselves using successful strategies. For example, even driving home after a staff meeting, one can mentally rehearse different responses to a situation that did not go well so that next time when an original intervention doesn't work, one can have a second or even third to try.

Proficient

Aikido Master George Leonard (1991) describes the level of *conscious competence* as the stage of deepest learning. It is energy intensive and tiring because the individual is making neurological and psychological adjustments. He is unlearning old patterns of responding. At this stage, learners may be tempted to give up practicing because the new application requires so much energy. For a while, learners may even be less effective than before. Persisting through the mechanical state of conscious competence is what builds essential routines. Moves are self-conscious, and others may notice or even criticize the practitioner. At this stage, it sometimes helps to declare your learning status and transform a stumble into a public learning opportunity.

Accomplished

Principles, skills, and strategies have been internalized so that the facilitator's moves appear effortless and effective. At this phase, mental energy is available to think several steps ahead, innovate with new approaches, and consider alternatives if what is tried does not work. This is a learning stage of refinement and experimentation as the facilitator moves beyond her boundaries.

Highly Accomplished/Expert

While the ultimate goal is to be excellent, helping others gain expertise may be even more of a goal. The most accomplished professionals have practiced for years and are conscious of their unconscious expertise; they are ready to teach others. The accomplished facilitator has perfected varied interventions that have become automatic and unconscious, bundling multiple moves to ensure smooth and seamless interventions. Think of a skilled musician who has not only memorized the music but shows passion, moving in ways that complement the music, movement that would have been unimaginable when she was still plunking away at scales. With conscious attention, this expert could also become an accomplished teacher.

PROFICIENCY SCALE

We have summarized the five levels of development in Figure 1.2 that will help the reader self-diagnose his level of skill development. We provide suggestions for how to improve at each level. This book is sequenced and designed to help a facilitator grow and learn. We also recommend some of our favorite references and Web sites. It is not always evident to facilitators that groups respond in direct correlation to the skill of the facilitator. When leaders fail to take responsibility for facilitation and appropriate interventions, groups will often flounder. Often the ineffective facilitator blames the group, creating a self-fulfilling prophecy. In our chaotic times, efficient use of time and emotional well-being are essential attributes for an organization. It is, therefore, a moral imperative for leaders to develop their ability to facilitate and intervene as appropriate.

ATTRIBUTES OF THE EXPERT

Facilitation is information intensive. Experts have for years cited George Miller's seminal 1956 research demonstrating that the human mind can hold just seven, plus or minus two, bits of

Figure 1.2 Locate Yourself on a Proficiency Scale

Consider how your skill level impacts the groups you work with. Consider a plan for your personal development.

Facilitator Stage	Facilitator Characteristics	Group Response	What You Can Do
Unaware	Lacks knowledge or information about facilitation or intervention skills. Passively accepts what happens in meetings as outside of her control. Attributes problems to others, not to leadership of the meeting.	Groups respond with frustration and report that meetings waste time, overwhelm them, have unproductive conflict, and often spin endlessly on topics of little value.	▪ Begin with reading Chapter 2: Preparing and Managing Nervousness. ▪ Read sequentially throughout the rest of the book. ▪ Acquire essential foundation knowledge of facilitation work by reading the seminal book *How to Make Meetings Work* by Doyle and Straus (1976), *Unlocking Group Potential for Improving Schools* by Garmston (2012), *Manager's Guide to Effective Meetings* by Streibel (2003), or *Best Practices for Facilitation* by Sibbet (2002).
Novice	Knows basic facilitation skills—how to get a group's attention, set focus and agenda, and manage transitions. May have difficulty leading decision-making processes.	Meeting tones are not consistent; sometimes the work goes well and other times it is stalled. This inconsistent positive reinforcement may give the illusion that	▪ Begin by reading Chapter 3: Intervention Principles to acquire insights about when to intervene and ways to go about it. ▪ Volunteer to facilitate portions of meetings to automate basic facilitation moves. ▪ Practice facilitation principles and moves when working with students. ▪ Observe colleagues. Take notes about their decisions and explore their thinking after the session.

Facilitator Stage	Facilitator Characteristics	Group Response	What You Can Do
	Sees the difficult participant as an impediment to progress and lacks skills to intervene effectively.	the group is more capable; however, when things get tough, the meeting breaks down. Groups blame a difficult person as the problem, and are not aware of any contribution they, as a group, might be making to problems. When the difficult person is absent, everyone notices how well the meeting went.	■ Cofacilitate and have a reflecting conversation afterward. ■ Facilitate and seek coaching. ■ Learn more about problem solving in groups and intervening by reading books such as *Unlocking Group Potential* by Garmston (2012), *Don't Just Do Something, Stand There! Ten Principles for Leading Meetings That Matter* by Weisbord and Janoff (2007), or *The Leader's Handbook: A Guide to Inspiring Your People and Managing the Daily Workflow* by Scholtes (1998).
Proficient	Has basic facilitation skills and can manage routine problems effortlessly in meetings. Views exceptional problems as challenges to	Groups perceive their meetings as effortless and may not attribute the success to the facilitator. However, when the facilitator is	■ Begin with reading Chapter 4: Deciding to Intervene. ■ View Focusing Four video to observe a master facilitator conducting a consensus session (Garmston & Dolcemascolo, 2009). ■ Schedule a planning conversation with a colleague prior to a difficult meeting and reflect with him or her after the session.

(Continued)

Figure 1.2 (Continued)

Facilitator Stage	Facilitator Characteristics	Group Response	What You Can Do
	solve over time. After a meeting reflects and learns by mentally revising the possible interventions and outcomes. Considers multiple options to employ should behaviors happen again.	absent they begin to notice a qualitative difference. A strong facilitator can become paternalistic keeping order, but not helping group members grow and learn. Groups can become dependent on the leader and stuck in their growth.	■ Seek every opportunity to practice and schedule a planning conversation with a colleague before the meeting and reflect with this person after the meeting. Become a facilitative participant in meetings you attend. This means you practice these skills when not the formally appointed leader. ■ Seek new references that have skill building information and read and envision how to apply the skills. Find an opportunity to practice. ■ Create a quick reference library with books such as *Thinker Toys: A Handbook of Business Creativity* by Michalko (1991), *The Presenter's Fieldbook: A Practical Guide* by Garmston (2005), or *Resonate: Present Visual Stories That Transform Audiences* by Duarte (2010).
Accomplished	Is able to respond, adapt, and improvise in the face of uncertainty. Sees self as responsible to the groups' success and does not blame	Groups report that they learn not only about how to do their job better but also how to work effectively with others. They begin to appreciate the quiet	■ Explore Chapters 4 through 7. ■ Learn from a master by reading books such as *The Skilled Facilitator* by Schwartz (2002). ■ Set specific goals for yourself such as using certain strategies should an opportunity arise, paraphrasing before taking new comments, or consciously applying one of the intervention principles found in Chapter 3.

Facilitator Stage	Facilitator Characteristics	Group Response	What You Can Do
	others. Consciously works to shift responsibility to the group and to teach the group about facilitation and intervention principles. Able to teach facilitation skills and interventions.	voice that finally speaks up or the loud voice that shows humility. They understand how dissenting views can be catalysts for deeper thinking. They transfer facilitation and intervention skills to other aspects of their life. Skilled facilitators quietly celebrate when they observe explicit carryover of skills used in one setting to another. For example a teacher might use paraphrasing as way to help students hold onto ideas, or a PLC member may use	■ Seek out colleagues with similar skill sets and collaborate on ideas. ■ Keep a facilitator's notebook with ideas, references, and reflections. ■ Join online community or follow a blog on organizational development. See list created by Terrence Seamon at http://learningvoyager.blogspot.com/2006/12/od-blogs-abound.html. ■ Seek opportunities to teach about facilitation and interventions. ■ Use first, second, third, and fourth point as a communication tool, as described in Chapter 6.

(Continued)

Figure 1.2 (Continued)

Facilitator Stage	Facilitator Characteristics	Group Response	What You Can Do
		outcome thinking to keep the group focused.	
Expert	Acts intuitively. Has many sets of linked steps that are performed unconsciously. Conscious of choices being made and could reveal the meta-cognition of facilitation to others. Regularly teaches the group about interventions using graphics, modeling, and third-point teaching.	Groups report that they are also learning to facilitate groups in effective ways. Members are increasingly willing to and capable of assuming leadership positions in this and other groups.	▪ Begin with Chapter 7: Strategies for Advanced Facilitation. Read earlier chapters as applicable. ▪ Learn about how stages of adult development affect decision making by reading books such as *Immunity to Change: How to Overcome It and Unlock the Potential in Yourself and Your Organization*, by Kegan and Lahey (2009). ▪ Teach, observe, and coach others.

information at a time. Newer research casts doubts on this idea. Nelson Corwin at the University of Missouri–Columbia states that most of us can handle just three to four pieces of information, depending on the complexity of the information, external conditions, and one's stress level (Rock, 2009).

Top facilitators learn to chunk information so that as they envision a move, they activate a series of linked steps that help create expert interventions. A colleague of ours, Kendall Zoller, advises facilitators to memorize the first five minutes of any interaction they plan with a group. Saying hello, establishing rapport, getting permission to facilitate, and framing the agenda all are routines within one chunk that could be named "start the meeting." These maps are created through experience and by embedding routine patterns through practice to levels of automaticity (unconscious competence).

Brain research has demonstrated that planning and monitoring behaviors occur in the frontal cortex and consume massive amounts of energy (Rock, 2009). By working to create automaticity, the facilitator can maximize brain energy and pay attention simultaneously to multiple variables. Skilled facilitators have routines for the five essentials for effective facilitation described in *Unlocking Group Potential* (Garmston, 2012).

We started this chapter with an example of an expert who recognized an outburst as threatening to the group, was able to ground himself, and worked directly with the situation. With his actions, he communicated in a way that the group learned that such outbursts would be handled safely and respectfully and that they would not be tolerated. Our expert facilitator demonstrated a clear intention to protect the group and a commitment to a larger theme—that the time spent together should be useful, positive, and productive. He communicated a deep respect for group members' right to dissent while also requiring the participant to become part of the solution.

SUMMARY

The journey from being unaware to expert is not just a matter of learning new intervention strategies. Reflection is the essential handmaiden to development through these stages. Experience alone is not our only teacher; rather, it is the reflective processes in which we engage that produces growth. Anticipating intervention needs, selecting and employing interventions, and then analyzing their effects are more important than having a range of interventions on which to draw. We have both learned by mentally revising our responses in a meeting that did not go smoothly, envisioning alternative and more successful responses. Experience has taught us that ineffective behavioral patterns repeat themselves, and the accomplished facilitator needs to be ready with a repertoire of response behavior sets. We have found that successful mental rehearsal is the best prescription—it builds personal confidence, and one of the hallmarks of the novice is anxiety about potential pitfalls. Appropriately, the next chapter looks in depth at the power of personal confidence. Confidence breeds competence.

2

BUILDING
PERSONAL
CONFIDENCE

In this chapter, we describe ways to manage the mind-body connection by monitoring one's internal states. These are always communicated in some way to the outside world, and this is particularly true when we are in front of groups, all eyes and ears on us. Readers will also find a number of experience-tested ideas to keep themselves functioning at their very best when unexpected problems arise, making sound facilitation moves essential to the group's success.

A facilitator who is uncomfortable with public speaking is less effective because fear and anxiety affect not only the level of facilitator confidence but also the level of trust the group has in the facilitator. A facilitator's quavering voice and excessive fidgeting or moving distract group members and split their attention. Some group members worry, "Is the facilitator OK?" They miss what is being said and become uneasy about the facilitator's leadership. Groups begin to lose confidence in the facilitator, and, over time, the efficacy of the group is eroded.

What is a facilitator to do?

Telling yourself to be confident and not to be nervous usually makes the feeling worse. However, reframing nervousness can help increase your feeling of security.

Believe that nervousness is there to support you. The Japanese martial art of aikido, literally translated as "the way of blending energy" (Crum, 1987), leads us to this understanding. From the perspective of aikido, all of life, including performance anxiety, is simply energy with which to dance. Nervous energy is a mental phenomenon with physiological results, and facilitators can achieve a desired state of calm through mental and physical preparation. As you gain experience, your need to consciously manage your nervousness will decrease. Mental rehearsal and practice help. In the last chapter, we reviewed the trajectory from novice to accomplished—knowing how, when, and why to intervene builds confidence. And of course, success breeds confidence.

CONNECTING MIND AND BODY

The body and mind are connected. Treating one addresses the other. To reframe nervousness, try tested physical and mental techniques (Garmston, 2005). As you practice these strategies, develop the personal patterns that best suit you.

1. Breathe

The first principle of public performance is to monitor and adjust your oxygen levels. The 3 1/2-pound mass we call a brain consumes 30% of the body's oxygen. When you experience stress, your breathing becomes shallow, and you hold your breath for brief periods. The neocortex in your brain, the site of language and reasoning, needs a full supply of oxygen to function. Stress instead shuttles precious oxygen to the limbic system to ready the body for survival.

The study of aikido and neurophysiology intersect at this point. The word *ki* in Japanese (*ch'i* in Chinese, *pneuma* in Greek, and *prana* in Sanskrit) comes from the notion of breath. Breath is considered the fundamental energy that connects all things and is the source of all creative action. The Eastern martial arts share this view. By controlling the flow of ki, the martial artist allegedly can achieve extraordinary powers.

2. Try Progressive Relaxation

Tense and then relax the muscles in your body, one area at a time. For example, first tense your toes and then relax them. Next, tense your feet and then relax them. Work your way up through your ankles, then calves, and so on.

3. Walk

Athletes walk and stretch before they enter the game. Walking and stretching warms up your muscles and also your psyche. Walking vigorously just prior to a presentation uses up adrenaline increases oxygen in the body, and relaxes the large muscles.

4. Center Yourself Physically

When you are centered, you become more in touch with who you are and depend less on outside approval. The centered state is simple, natural, and powerful.

To center yourself do the following:

- ■ Stand.
- ■ Allow both your arms to drop naturally to your sides.

- Spread your feet so that they are appropriately balanced beneath your shoulders.
- Take several long, deep breaths.
- With each slow exhalation, imagine the tension flowing out of your body from head to toe.
- Allow your spine to lengthen; mentally reach toward your hair and pull a strand of it up so that your neck is elongated and your spine is comfortably stretched.
- Imagine wearing a heavy overcoat causing your shoulders to relax.
- Now, from this position, sway slightly back and forth for 10 to 15 seconds, gradually decreasing the size of the sway until you reach center.
- Next, imagine that you are pushing both feet into the floor, and then release that tension.

Your body will let you know when you have a centered feeling from which you can present at your best. Crum (1987) has additional methods for centering yourself.

One source of stress is lack of experience. The next three strategies help overcome inexperience.

5. Over Prepare. Over Prepare

Over prepare. Redirecting butterflies begins with planning. Pay careful attention to allocating time as you develop the meeting agenda and provide appropriate strategies for group tasks during the meeting. Get very clear and specific about what you will say in your opening comments. If this is a special occasion and you feel particularly nervous, memorize the first seven minutes so that you can deliver the lines even if you close down mentally. In particular, be clear about how you will describe yourself and your role, the meeting outcomes, the opening inclusion activity, and any comments you will make about the agenda. Plan to stand still during the opening so people can take your measure. Anticipate potential problem spots in the meeting and be prepared with some intervention approaches.

6. Address the Stress of Conflict

When things go wrong when you're driving, the car's tires lose traction on the pavement and slide into a skid. The smallest adjustment of the wheel or tap on the brakes can bring the vehicle under control—or spin it off into mayhem.

As a facilitator, you must first take care of yourself and maintain personal equilibrium to access your supreme "driving" skills. The algebra teacher's outburst described in Chapter 1 threatened both the facilitator and the group. The teacher's angry voice introduced anger and conflict into the meeting room. Anger exacerbates conflict and triggers a sense of being physically or psychologically endangered. Psychological danger includes threats to self-esteem or dignity, perceived unfairness, insults, the sense of being demeaned, or perceived futility. Perceived danger triggers a limbic surge, and public anger creates the same surge in the facilitator, causing a quick rush of energy (caused by a release of catecholamine) that ripples through the nervous system and creates a general unease that can persist as long as the meeting lasts (Garmston, 1998).

All conflict begins internally, and learning productive ways of working with conflict is a lifelong task. The best teacher is reflection and access to healthy models. While many books outline strategies for conflict resolution, negotiating for success, winning arguments, and building a win-win consensus, the strongest foundation for addressing conflicting energies with dignity and effectiveness is simple but not simplistic, clear but not easy, a starting point but not complete: Take care of yourself.

Don't get too hungry, too tired, or too lonely. Balance your emotional portfolio in work, family, recreational, and spiritual pursuits—and be grounded.

Listen with your ears, eyes, and heart. Listening may be your greatest asset as a facilitator. Henry Kissinger used to say that during his shuttle diplomacy periods, he would remember his humanity and remind himself to forget his agenda. Michael Doyle, codeveloper of the interaction method of managing meetings, advised declining any invitations to lunch with the group during a difficult facilitation setting. Protect your energy, and gear up for the next round.

Our Adaptive Schools work teaches us to presume positive intentions and to maintain generosity of spirit (Garmston & Wellman, 2013). Remind yourself that almost all behaviors are motivated by positive intention—people trying to take care of and protect themselves. Do not overthink others' intentions. Remember the following:

- People (even you) are rarely as benevolent as they perceive themselves to be.
- Others are rarely as evil as their opponents perceive them to be.
- People rarely spend as much time thinking about the issues as is assumed.
- Others' behaviors are rarely planned or thought out.
- Most aspects of conflict are not the result of coldhearted calculation but have spun off from prior events.

- Previous patterns and past judgments taint present perceptions.
- Every conflict has a history.
- Pretend as though even the most outlandish behaviors are simply attempts to take care of one's self.

When you have trouble remembering these positive intentions or find yourself judging others, take a step away from both the group and yourself. We call this act of stepping aside "going to the balcony" because the move is meant to allow the facilitator to take in the whole picture as if from a balcony, disassociating from the group momentarily to gain a deeper understanding of the interactions and to assess positive intentions.

We often hear our friend Laura Lipton asking us, "What is your most generous interpretation of the situation?" By taking care of yourself and assuming a larger viewpoint, you will be better able to assess your repertoire of intervention strategies and focus on the group's needs—rather than on protecting yourself.

7. Check Your Negative Predictions at the Door

It is easy to become caught up in what might be rather than live in the present. Doing so causes anxiety, and if you are anxious, this uncomfortable feeling transmits itself to the group. If you catch yourself worrying that you will not be able to respond appropriately to an objection if it comes up, notice the thought, take a breath, and let it go. If you realize you are worried you might fail, or not do something as elegantly as you would like, notice this inner dialogue and let yourself get curious, rather than apprehensive about what is coming next. Change your thought—"I will do fine"—to change your emotion, and then focus on the present, and just observe, rather than react to limiting inner dialogue. It does not need to control your emotions.

8. When Stuck, Move

Therapists have long known that when a client is stuck, just physically moving will help to begin to open their thinking. If you notice a feeling of panic that you do not know what to do or that you are being attacked, stop, take a deep breath, and move to a new space. Sometimes it is important to let the group know that you are changing direction. You might say, "Let's try doing something different," or "Let me see if I can say it a different way."

9. Maintain Your Identity as a Facilitator

It is easy to lose focus and to want to solve the problem with the group. You can avoid being caught up in the group's drama by remembering that your job is to help the group maintain its focus, to keep participants' energy high, and to help members engage in their best thinking. The accomplished facilitator knows that each individual group member and the group itself must solve their own problems.

Be in charge of your emotional state. While being rested and well fed helps you keep your emotional balance, these factors alone are not enough. We learned from John Grinder (1990, personal communication) that when someone acts out in a group, you can be defensive, or you can choose to be curious and ask yourself, "What might be causing that behavior?" In reality, much clumsy and even hurtful behavior can be attributed to the person's lack of effective communication skills.

Find the best way for you to stay centered when some aspect of your identity is challenged. Know what belief systems trigger your judgments and remember, at those times, to observe from the balcony. Don't let your response to others color your ability to facilitate. Intervene with neutrality.

Because we are evolutionarily wired to be defensive, we tend to read negative intentions into behavior and react without thinking. Successfully intervening in a group requires that you become conscious of these deeply embedded survival behaviors and learn new routines to monitor your internal state. Presume positive intentions.

Part of maintaining control is knowing your styles and dispositions. Do you need to be liked? Need to be in charge? We all have some of those qualities. Know your cognitive style—are you oriented toward big pictures or small details? Do you like things to be linear and sequential or random and abstract? Sometimes a group member or a facilitator who spends too much time feeding his stylistic needs, such as compulsively zeroing in on minute details or jumping around with no apparent order, can elicit annoyance.

10. Monitor Your Need to Know

Remember, like a personal trainer, to be clear that the client is to do the work. Manage your curiosity about elements of what is said. Probe for specificity if you notice the group does not understand, and do not probe because you want to know more. Bob once facilitated a statewide technology group for a period of several years. Most of the time the conversation was over his head, yet he had not been asked to facilitate because of his knowledge of topic; rather, he was there because of his process knowledge.

11. Take Care to Arrange the Room

Paying attention to the physical aspects of the environment helps the facilitator to be fully present. No detail is too small.

This includes precutting small strips of masking tape for hanging flip chart paper to avoid the distraction of having to search for the tape in the heat of the meeting, slowing the meeting's momentum.

The ideal meeting room is quiet, comfortable, has empty wall space where the group can post its work, and is free from distractions. Furniture, space, and visual displays all can mediate thinking and behavior. Visual displays are important for working groups—of the 11 million bits of information bombarding people each second, 10 million are received through the eyes. Of all that information, we process only 40% consciously (The Sound Learning Centre Limited, n.d.). Furthermore, when people get tired, their capacity to process information auditorially is the first to diminish, creating a greater need for visual cues.

Specific tasks and group work require consciously attending to the room's arrangement and to providing materials. Room arrangement communicates and provides structures for the interactions you desire. Be sure charting materials such as markers, tape, pads, and sturdy flip charts are readily available. Consider what wall space is available for group members to post charts as they work. High-performing groups post charts that state outcomes and that remind members about working agreements, meeting standards, and other group-member agreements. High-performing groups capture their work on charts (or interactive whiteboards) to create a working memory of discussions and to assure that their work is efficiently carried over from meeting to meeting. Group memory and graphic processes support learning and retention and are expedient.

A poor environment can derail a meeting as certainly as a disruptive participant. Appendix A offers tips for arranging a room.

12. Create a Circle of Excellence

Think of a time when you were in front of a group and felt successful or someone complimented you on your work.

- Envision that experience fully: See the room as from your eyes, not as an outsider looking in; see the people, feel your body in that room, and notice the internal sensations associated with that success.
- Practice bringing this success framework up at will, perhaps by mentally rehearsing it at night as you go to sleep. Make sure you feel the success in your muscle memory.
- Prior to the meeting, arrive early to have the space to yourself. Stand in the spot you will use for most of the meeting and envision your success framework. Once you can feel it in your body memory, gradually expand the feeling so it encompasses the room. This new space is your circle of excellence.

SUMMARY

Whether a novice or an expert, facilitators must understand themselves and monitor their internal states so they can better serve the group. Facilitators who are grounded model respect, integrity, and dignity, even under the most difficult circumstances. Most important, what we model is mirrored back to us from the group. Paradoxically, until you take care of yourself, you really cannot help others. In the next chapter, we begin to describe fundamental intervention principles that all accomplished facilitators will want to adopt. Internalized principles guide quick decisions in stressful situations and model values. This next chapter allows both the novice and the expert to calibrate their ability to walk their talk.

3

INTERVENTION PRINCIPLES

E very group offers a new experience, requiring that the skilled facilitator have a schema for organizing interventions. Nimble facilitators organize their thinking around internal principles, which they consider before intervening. In a sense, these rules of thumb serve as general guides. As in teaching, the metacognition of the practitioner informs the choices made in the moment. When principles are clear, decisions are easier and can override the anxiety a facilitator might feel in disruptive situations. In this chapter, we review the fundamental principles of effective intervention.

Expert facilitators learn to understand when and how to intervene by applying intervention principles. These include compassion, language precision, congruence, and intervening initially at levels of low risk, before increasing the directness of the intervention. The goal is always to help participants feel safe and stay focused on the work at hand, even as a disruptive event is being redirected. Sometimes interventions must become increasingly direct, focusing on problem behaviors, which can raise the discomfort level for individuals and the group. The greater the facilitator's experience with intervening, the more creative and inventive she becomes.

The ideas here have worked for us in particular contexts and are not the right answers for every situation, but they are options to consider. You will have other ideas and principles of intervention that have worked for the particular challenges you have faced, and we encourage you to develop your personalized set of intervention principles, perhaps even combining the strategies to develop complex heuristics for intervention.

PRINCIPLES GUIDE DECISIONS

Accomplished facilitators use interventions to develop the group. Effective groups that meet regularly reach a mature stage when they learn over time to be self-monitoring, reflective, and self-corrective. Groups reach this advanced stage when skilled facilitators choose interventions that mediate and enhance the group's capacity to learn from experience.

Rather than setting rules, which tend to be more specific and less flexible, the facilitator is better served by following some general principles that guide the group's interaction. Some principles described in *Unlocking Group Potential* (Garmston, with von Frank, 2012) are the following:

- Maintain maximum focus on task.
- Use the least time possible to make corrections—be quick; be elegant; be effective.

While most rules once were principles, rules become confining. For example, while Chapter 4 stresses the need to create working agreements, formal agreements can become overworked and rigid if care is not taken to avoid using them robotically.

Excellent facilitation requires flexibility and improvisation. Each group is different, and nothing is appropriate for every group or all settings. To make the best choice for a group, a facilitator must sometimes apply out-of-the-box thinking and know when and how stringently to apply a principle.

Keep the following four principles firmly embedded in your approach.

Compassion

Our most important advice for working in a difficult situation is to be compassionate. Socrates argued that no one deliberately chooses to do something to harm himself or knowingly rejects that which would benefit him most. Yet we have all seen examples of what appears to be self-defeating behaviors or comments that distract from a person's ability to be heard or to influence others. In our experience, even when someone's choice seems preposterous, the individual truly is making the best choice he has available at the time.

As facilitators, we also make the best choices we have available. When both a facilitator and a group, for whatever reason, perceive that they have limited choices, the road becomes riskier and sometimes disastrous. High-risk situations make players—facilitator and members—vulnerable to emotionally charged decisions in which group members may retreat or lash out, blaming others for the problem. When the atmosphere becomes toxic like this, the facilitator must dip into stores of compassion, observing without judgment and forgiving herself and others.

Precise Language

Most facilitator interventions are routine: steering a conversation, creating a visual focus, redirecting energy, and giving directions. The skilled facilitator learns how and when to use specific language. For example, see the following:

- Use descriptive (someone is having a side conversation) rather than judgmental words (someone is being rude). Ground your language with examples of what can be seen or heard.
- Use words that are specific in their reference. Refer to each subgroup in terms that reflect its independent identity (parents) rather than in broader terms that use another subgroup as a point of reference (nonteachers).
- Take the focus off of yourself. Rather than saying, "I would like you to . . ." or "Please look at me," say, "Please pause and turn so you can see and hear one another," or "Please turn toward the chart listing your agreements."
- Use the active voice paired with specific names. For example, say, "Judy decided to include the data from last year," rather than "It was decided to include the data from last year."

Sense when to use a name. For example, when a group refers to an administrator by title or a collective descriptor, such as "the district office" rather than a proper noun, the group is practicing some level of avoidance. So paraphrase and prompt the group to say "Linda" rather than "she," or "Tom" rather than "the administrator," or "Floyd and Leo" instead of "the district office." You might ask a direct question such as, "To whom are you referring when you say, 'the administration?'"

- ■ Maintain role clarity by using pronouns that describe your position and relationship to the group. For example, if you are external to the group, refer to "your work" when discussing the group's activities. If you are internal, identify the work as "our work."

- ■ Use emotionally neutral labels. It is usually safest to discuss emotionally charged work by disassociating the work from the emotional target and applying the most neutral terms, such as "the work" or "this task" rather than "low test scores." Depersonalize the task to make it psychologically safer for group members to engage with the idea rather than the person or group.

- ■ Teach and insist on the principle of balancing paraphrasing, inquiry, and advocacy, perhaps reminding groups that the most effective groups focus on others more than selves and have a one-to-one inquiry to advocacy ratio. Too often groups deteriorate to a few verbose members arguing over viewpoints, with the majority of the group sitting by as silent onlookers. When groups learn to use dialogue principles of paraphrasing and inquiry before moving to advocacy, they often clear up misunderstandings or find new points of view. Some groups turn this in to a working agreement and create a posted graphic as a reminder, such as in Figure 3.1.

Figure 3.1   Balancing Advocacy

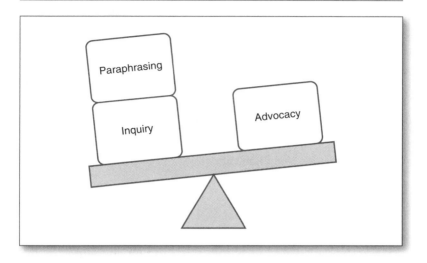

Congruence

Facilitators must walk their talk. For example, if they enforce a standard of one voice in the room at a time, then they should not talk over the group. Skilled facilitators monitor their body language, message, and actions for congruence. Using proper voice tone is an example. An effective facilitator needs to decide whether his intent is to send (be credible) or to receive information (invite response). The posture of credibility is characterized by placing the feet parallel and hip-distance apart; holding arms perpendicular or parallel to the ground; breathing abdominally, calmly, and deeply; and standing still (Zoller, 2010).

Grinder (1993) describes two voice registers that send different messages: one that invites comment and the other that gives a command, and does not invite negotiation. A voice tone, which goes up and down, is considered approachable as it invites the listener to respond. This *approachable voice* encourages participation. However, when the speaker uses a more narrow, flatter pitch range and drops the voice at the end, the listener perceives a voice of command or direction, and knows she is expected to agree. Grinder calls this a *credible voice* because the audience believes that this speaker knows what she is talking about. Facilitators use this voice when wanting to be definitive, when giving directions, and to establish credibility. When intervening, the facilitator will want to consider the intent and then choose appropriate voice. Zoller (2010) describes this nuance:

> Each of us has a range in voice pitch that can be used effectively depending on the intended outcome. Our voice pitch can be consciously selected based on our deliberate intention. By changing our voice tone, we can change the meaning of the words and influence the perceptions of the listeners. (p. 3)

Accomplished facilitators alternate between these two voice registers.

From Low to High Risk

Accomplished facilitators ask, "What is the risk of intervening?" and "How can I strategically minimize the risk with early intervention?" Schwartz (2002) suggests a three-tiered ladder of interventions starting with lowest risk and moving to higher.

A. State issues, problems, and challenges as abstractions. This is the safest level of intervention for the group and facilitator and places the conversation "out there" in the abstract and hypothetical. By not referencing the behavior or person, the facilitator reduces the group's tendency toward defensiveness. See the following examples:

■ "When more than one conversation is occurring at the same time, it is difficult for everyone to hear," rather than, "Your talking is making it difficult . . ."
■ "And [instead of 'but,' you might say] here is another perspective."

Notice the subtle nuance added with "and." The word "but" is perceived as refuting the preceding statement, whereas "and" is perceived as adding information.

B. Report observations of behavior. The facilitator and the group as a whole must have a measure of trust and rapport for this to be a safe and effective level of intervention. The observation alone then may be enough to raise awareness and change the behavior. Sometimes you may wish to follow the observation with an inquiry to deepen awareness of the dynamic and use the situation as a teaching opportunity.

■ "Whoops! Hang on. There are several conversations going on right now."
■ "Notice that since the morning break, you've had contributions from nearly everyone. That is one of the goals you set for yourself."
■ "Yesterday you agreed to disagree agreeably. Here is a snapshot from this meeting. In the last interchange, several statements were made that presumed negative motivation from other group members. How can you state concerns without the negative edge?"

C. Ask questions intended to illuminate perceptions. At this level of intervention, you help members articulate both thinking and feeling, delving beneath the surface of group behaviors and inviting the group to consider the sources of the behavior. Timing and respectful phrasing are important. These moves must be made with an approachable voice.

- "People seem tired. Do you want to take a break, or do you want to push on for 15 minutes?"
- "How is the group doing on its norm of listening to one another? Tell your partner." Then ask the group to share reports.
- "At least half the group is engaging in side talk. Is that OK with you?" Seek the group's input to modify the behaviors.

Schwartz (2002) recommends a further refinement to the third principle and describes how to ask questions with more precision along a continuum of low to high risk. Figure 3.2 is organized from safer to higher risk.

Figure 3.2   Lowest to Highest Risk Questioning Interventions

Perceptions about the following	Sample language
Roles or Functions	■ "What do you want a recorder to do and not do?" ■ "What agreements would you like to make about how you will work today?"
Performance (Focusing on results)	■ "What's your degree of satisfaction with getting work done this morning?"

Perceptions about the following	Sample language
	■ "May I see a show of fingers—five as a high to one as low—with how OK you are with our progress so far?"
Process (Focusing on work behavior and relationships, e.g., meeting standards, norms, and agreements)	■ "What's happening here? What are you noticing?" ■ "What's your sense of where you are in a decision-making process?" ■ "What are some of the decisions you made about when and how to participate? What were some of the effects of your decisions on yourself and the group?"
Interpersonal (Focusing on honest, constructive expressions of feelings often kept hidden)	■ "How do you feel about the group when people are interrupting each other?" ■ "How do you feel about your goal of respectful listening?"
Intrapersonal (Focusing on raising consciousness about personal behaviors and the effect of behaviors on the group)	■ "Mark, what might be some reasons that you end up in conflicts more frequently than other group members?" ■ "Shelly, can you help the group understand what leads you to fairly consistently take a position opposing what is being talked about?"

SUMMARY

An essential step in the journey from novice to expert is to internalize these and other personal principles consistent with the facilitator's experience and knowledge. They become the foundation on which facilitators guide groups through unsettling times. When principles are internalized and automatic, they become the fabric of how we facilitate, so much so that they create our personal fingerprint. For example, we share a personal principle related to a goal of helping groups be efficacious and in charge of their learning. At the beginning of a session, we suggest that members say, "Louder please," when they cannot hear a member's contribution. We guide the group in a choral response. Later, when someone complains to us they could not hear, we ask what they should say. This prompt is intended to remind them that they are not dependent on the facilitator but are in charge of their experience. When principles are personal and part of our identity, they become natural and congruent ways in which others can and will expect us to respond. In the next chapter, we will delve into the basic elements or rules of intervention.

4

DECIDING TO INTERVENE

B y definition, the facilitator is in charge of process. In this chapter, we provide practical tips for facilitators to learn to walk their talk, employing principles they have internalized to guide their interaction with groups. The facilitator's clarity about outcomes is the basis for effective effort. We often tell groups that there are three criteria for successful meetings: clear outcomes, clear outcomes, and clear outcomes. We say this to make a point that often is given lip service but is less often practiced.

Facilitators carefully consider when to intervene, recognizing that some anomalies in the group process can be ignored in the moment. Skilled facilitators will ask themselves if it is necessary to intervene, and if so, can it be quick, can it be done protecting the dignity of the group, and can the group learn from it. Being clear about outcomes helps the facilitator anticipate and often preclude problems by keeping the group working effectively. To intervene successfully the facilitator needs to be clear about meeting standards, working agreements, and factors such as relevance, energy, and group emotions. The overarching outcomes for any meeting are that participants are focused, energized, resourceful, and feel psychologically safe so they can accomplish work. Facilitators help the group establish these conditions and intervene when those outcomes are threatened. This consciousness assists the facilitator in anticipating and precluding problems. This chapter describes how to consider these preemptive moves.

Facilitators establish credibility and gain permission to intervene by their self-confident handling of basic meeting procedures. Permission to intervene is also granted when members trust that the facilitator is going to work nonjudgmentally with the group and refrain from engaging in topics the group is discussing. One might think of gum chewing, in which gum is the content of the meeting and chewing the processes by which the group does its work, the facilitator is responsible for chewing.

You intervene when you delay calling on a person, use proximity to quiet a talker, or ask for someone who has not talked to comment. Processes are activities such as brainstorming, pairs sharing, lineups, or jigsaws. When introducing processes in which the group is to engage, the facilitator employs the *what-why-how* pattern. While each part of the message is important, "the why"— the rationale for the process—is most important. When members understand the reasons for a process—how it will serve them— potential resistance is reduced and participation is more purposeful. For multistep directions, the "how" is supported visually. We often give all three as follows (Garmston, 2002):

- What—"The next step is to brainstorm."
- Why—"As you know, the purpose of brainstorming is to get as many ideas on the table as possible. Questions or comments derail the process leading to a more limited and less useful list."

■ How—"I will record the ideas on this chart paper. When you raise your hand, I will give you a number to place you in a queue so you know you will have a turn and not worry about being able to add your idea. If you have a question or comment, hang on to it. We will come back to it at the next step."

ESTABLISH MEETING STANDARDS

Begin by establishing expectations for excellence. In a now seminal work, Michael Doyle and David Straus (1976) investigated the question, "What is the minimum number of meeting standards a group must know and follow for the group to be on task, take the minimum time to reach its objectives, and for members to have high levels of satisfaction?" They identified five essential standards:

■ Group members discuss only one topic at a time.
■ Members use only one process at a time.
■ Participation in the meeting is balanced.
■ Conflict about ideas is encouraged, but affective conflict is eliminated.
■ Group members understand and agree on meeting roles— typically facilitator, recorder, group member, and person with role or knowledge authority (Garmston & Wellman, 2009, 2013).

These standards—and how to introduce, practice, and monitor them—are explored in *Unlocking Group Potential* (Garmston, 2012).

Once group members understand the standards, they know that the facilitator has permission to intervene should the group not follow the standards. For example, if the group is discussing the topic of program assessment and one person brings up report cards, the facilitator has group members' implicit permission to intervene. The facilitator might use a relevance inquiry and say, "Help us understand how that idea connects to our topic," while pointing to the agenda item. In another case, perhaps a member begins to ask questions during a brainstorming session. The facilitator can use a stop-redirect move, saying, "Please hold on to that thought. We will have time later for questions."

SET WORKING AGREEMENTS

Another area for clarity is around working agreements. When working with an ad hoc group, suggest a set of predetermined working agreements, such as those listed in Figure 4.1, and ask if the group is willing to adopt them. If you have the gift of a long-term relationship, the group can develop their own working agreements; the list in Figure 4.1 can be used as a starting place.

Figure 4.1   Sample Agreements and Standards

Working Agreements	Meeting Standards
■ **Demonstrate mutual respect.** Respect people and ideas. Respecting others does not equate to agreeing with them. ■ **Employ skillful listening.** Seek first to understand, then to be understood. ■ **Develop sufficient consensus.** Work to understand all views, distinguish between dialogue and discussion, give each person an equal voice, and reach 80% agreement of those present to constitute consensus.	■ Address one topic at a time. ■ Use one process at a time. ■ Balance participation. ■ Value cognitive conflict. ■ Understand and agree on roles.

When agreements are well established, the group understands that, once set, these agreements are not negotiable and the facilitator will seek every opportunity to ensure compliance while working to shift more responsibility to the group. When the group becomes the keeper of the agreements, most problems disappear.

Without exception, those that take the time to set, monitor, and evaluate working agreements report that monitoring working agreements and intervening when needed is one of the most important strategies for improving the group's work. Groups too often set working agreements only to cut corners in subsequent meetings. They seldom take time to review these agreements or to self-evaluate. After all, schools are busy places, with conflicting agendas and a finite amount of meeting time. Furthermore, when the group work seems smooth, it seems unnecessary—or even a waste of time—to review the agreements.

However, when agreements are violated, the facilitator is faced with having to decide whether to intervene. When the facilitator ignores the petty violations and hopes that the behaviors will magically disappear at the next meeting, the problems tend to grow. Worse yet, not intervening reinforces an uneven norm—some people follow the working agreements while others do not. Although the erosion begins with just a few cases, violations can become contagious. Once an agreement has been violated, it becomes easier and easier for group members to continue violating it, reminding us of the need for facilitators to build in vigilant monitoring of working agreements.

A principal once told how in a fit of frustration at the end of a meeting, he chided his staff, "I need to remind you of our working agreement, 'One conversation at a time.' We had too many side conversations today, and we need to work on this." After the meeting, one of his most faithful teachers approached him and apologized for not following the agreement. No one else said a thing. Several years later, as he looked back, this principal realized that the one teacher whom he had never considered the problem carried the guilt for the group. By not asking his staff to evaluate their behaviors in relation to their agreements, he had failed to follow through, which caused a gradual reversion to old habits. In hindsight, the principal commented, "Without realizing it, by ignoring the behaviors, I sanctioned a new agreement—that it was okay to show up with less commitment to pay attention."

Once rules are established, the facilitator must make sure that working agreements are followed. From time to time, individuals might need to violate a rule by leaving early or taking an emergency phone call; as long as deviations are outside of the norm, no one will care. When bad habits become the de facto working agreement, everyone notices.

The facilitator's role at every meeting is to publicly and privately pay conscious attention to resetting working agreements. Consistency should be the norm, not the exception. The payoff is that routines can be shortened and will become more efficient and the group will have a set of behaviors and procedures to fall back on. Posted working agreements are useful reminders, and the facilitator can reference them with a gesture, without saying a word. We sometimes include the working agreements on the printed meeting agenda.

Recalibrate Using a *Complete Message*

When a facilitator has the privilege of working with the same group over time, taking time to recalibrate or solve problems around working agreements can be beneficial. We have found that a valuable intervention strategy is the structured *complete message*. When giving information that others may not want to hear, it is essential to be clear, concise, and complete. It is also important to neutralize emotions.

We adapted this move first described to us years ago in a book for psychologists called *Messages: The Communication Book* (McKay, Davis, & Fanning, 1983). We use a modified version of this sequence that outlines four steps:

1. Express observations

2. Express thoughts

3. Express feelings

4. Express needs as a direction

We suggest writing each part and practicing in advance. Practice is essential to make sure that your tone of voice is neutral and does not betray any latent frustration or anger at the group for not keeping agreements. The stronger your feelings about a problem, the more likely, without self-monitoring, you will taint the message with non-verbal body language that shows judgment.

This recalibration can be quick in the form of a reminder or take about 15 to 20 minutes if the group is asked to problem solve. When the facilitator involves the group in recalibrating, participants create the solution and so their commitment to solving the problem is high. Engaging the entire group also harnesses the power of positive role models to create elegant solutions.

The process might look like this:

■ State the data: "At the last meeting, five people were late. Today, six people were late."

■ Restate the rule: "Our working agreements states, 'Be on time.'"

(Continued)

(Continued)

- Query: "I am wondering what we can put in place to help *everyone* be here on time?"
- Solve the problem as a group: "Turn to a partner and talk about what helps *you* be here on time, every time."
- Keep track of ideas on a chart—a neutral third position—that all can see.

Groups we have worked with have generated a number of creative solutions: Give a seven-minute "all call" before the meeting, come four minutes early, have an "on time" buddy pick up a "tardy buddy," talk privately with latecomers, and review arrival time data after two months.

When using this process with a group, the facilitator is advised to craft the *complete message* in writing in advance, immediately after the meeting, so that the data are accurate and the message is congruent and proactive—it deals with the problem when it is fresh. Once written, the message is ready for the next meeting, one week or a month later.

Evaluate Working Agreements

For many facilitators, evaluating working agreements is a challenge. Don't call for an evaluation only when a few violate the ground rules. There is nothing a group resents more than being held accountable for a few irresponsible people. Ideally, design regular procedures that shift the burden so that the group becomes the standards bearer, and if one or two people have violated the agreements, the facilitator can deal with the issue privately. In one example, we were working with probation officers, and two were horsing around with each other, disturbing other members of the group. At break time, we invited them to talk with us about the situation. We told them that we knew their intention was to contribute to the group and simultaneously have a good time. However, we informed them that they may not know the perceptions of others in the group. Others, we said, thought they were trying to disrupt the situation and were annoyed with them. That was all that needed to be said. After break and for the rest of the meeting they were model citizens.

Public evaluation makes the group responsible for monitoring members' behavior, a desirable end goal. Make the data from group evaluations public. Written evaluations require more commitment than verbal reflections. When follow through might be a problem, we recommend written evaluations. The facilitator is responsible for following up—nothing is more irritating than being asked to complete an evaluation that is never mentioned again. Routines should be built in to agenda setting to assure to working agreements are attended to and evaluated from time to time.

Often, leaders complain about the lack of time for evaluations. To save time, especially with a larger group, capture feedback with short end-of-meeting surveys, and then analyze the data with a small subgroup. Examples of these can be found at www.thinkingcollaborative.com and in the companion book by Garmston with von Frank (2012). Another way to save time at the end of each meeting is to evaluate only one or two agreements at a time, reviewing all the agreements over time. Results of subgroup work should be used to set the working agreement priorities for the next meeting. When work is done in committee, publish it and link it to the main agenda for the next meeting.

If You Are the Principal

While we advise principals to develop others in the group to perform the facilitation function, there are occasions in which the principal does choose to facilitate (Garmston & Wellman, 2009, 2013). Even when the principal is a group member and has delegated the facilitation role to others, she still can provide leadership in regular evaluation of the group's effectiveness at working together. Here are examples of two very different ways of accomplishing this.

In one school, the principal ended each meeting by eliciting public feedback and capturing it on a simple, large T-chart, listing what worked well on the left and what still needed work on the right. Before adjourning, the principal asked staff to identify one working agreement to improve on. This saved her time at the next meeting because the "working agreement reminder" would be listed at the top of the new agenda and briefly reviewed at the beginning of the meeting (e.g., "Working Agreement Focus for Today: One Conversation at a Time").

In another school, the principal used a simple, numbered Likert scale that participants used to rate how effectively the group followed the working agreements, from "not at all" to "all the time." Initially, the ratings were collected anonymously and tabulated publicly, with quality time set aside for discussing the data.

He chose this method because two teachers routinely dominated the discussions, and he was afraid his quieter teachers would not be willing to publicly confront this behavior. He remembers the day when the teachers were asked to evaluate the balance of voices in the room. The data came in showing that 100% of the teachers had judged their performance as less than favorable—few voices had been heard. His open-ended query was, "So what happened today?"

There was a long pause and then one brave, quiet teacher said, "I did not feel that anyone listened to me the last time I talked, so I keep quiet." Another one piped in and said, "I only talk if I really care about the solution. Today I did not care how it came out."

The discussion that followed was a frank exposé about why some participants did not speak up. Finally, one of the most verbose teachers publicly acknowledged, "Sometimes I get so frustrated when no one talks that I just have to jump in. I need to try to let others talk first."

The principal commented later, "Privately I was cheering. This conversation far exceeded my expectations. At our next meeting, we had what we needed—a balance of voices in the room."

Michael Doyle and David Straus (1976), codevelopers of the interaction method of running meetings, call reviewing working agreements *going slow to go fast.* While building in routines initially takes time, the group learning and commitment to well-run meetings makes the time and effort worthwhile. Garmston and Wellman (2009, 2013) note that any group too busy to self-assess is too busy to improve. Reflection, not experience alone, is our teacher.

CLARIFY TASKS

Meetings have tasks to accomplish; in successful meetings, the participants understand and are clear about the tasks. Accomplished facilitators define tasks on the agenda using specific verbs. They also know when to have the group clarify the task and who will have the authority to make the final decision. Groups will suffer morale problems when decision-making processes and authority are not clear. Group members must know if they are to decide, recommend, inform, explore, or construct. The facilitator's responsibility is to make the group's role clear and to clarify this role when needed.

However, just saying it does not ensure the group knows it. The facilitator may find it valuable to check the group's understanding of the task before proceeding with the deliberations. A high school instructional leadership team once took 40 minutes to clarify the task given to them by the principal. Initially, the task seemed clear: "Recommend the degree of autonomy that professional learning teams should have in determining the focus for instructional improvement." The issues were complex enough that the team ended up needing a lengthy conversation to be clear about the task.

Task as Given/Task as Understood (TAG/TAU)

One process facilitators use to help the group clarify tasks is called TAG/TAU for task as given, task as understood. In this process, the facilitator describes the process to be used in a credible voice. He might say, "The task today is for each professional learning team to decide on a priority focus." Then stepping to a new space, in an approachable voice, he might ask members, "What do you each understand the task to be?"

Intervene as Necessary

Choosing a strategy to use as a facilitator in a difficult situation is often easier than deciding whether to intervene at all—or when. Skilled facilitators must sense when a group needs a nudge in a different direction, taking the mood of the group and anticipating potential problems. Experience is the best teacher for knowing when to intervene. However, asking yourself a few key questions can guide you in gaining that valuable experience.

Deciding to Intervene With an Ad Hoc Group

Interventions for ad hoc groups need to be nuanced as facilitator–group relationships and patterns have not been established. More often than not, in short-term groups, small distractions are best ignored. Phones, texting, and laptops are 21st-century distractions, so decide in advance to state the norm up front or be prepared to ignore it. Because of the short-term nature of the relationship, minor violations may need to be ignored. Ask yourself the following questions:

- Is it appropriate to intervene?
- Is the behavior distracting to members of the group, or is it irritating me?
- Will my intervention take more time than I have?
- Will my intervention distract from the tasks to be done?
- Did I identify the offending activity clearly at the beginning of the meeting?
- Can the group learn from it, or will it distract them from the task?

When the facilitator is working with a group over time, the decision to intervene has different, more long-term consequences. In these cases, the facilitator needs to be preemptive or be prepared for a more direct intervention. Failure to intervene inadvertently sanctions the behavior the facilitator wants to extinguish.

INTERVENING PREEMPTIVELY

Facilitators often can predict and preempt the need for an intervention. The facilitator can generally foresee issues that lead to the need to intervene, issues of relevance, fatigue, emotion, and conflict and, with foresight and planning, choose meeting structures and strategies to diminish the potential negative effect of these distractions.

Anticipate the issues and prepare for them by continually asking yourself these questions:

1. Is the Agenda Relevant?

Set an agenda of items that will engage the group, and pay attention to pacing. In classrooms, teachers find that their need to manage the group is directly proportional to the quality and relevance of the lesson. The same is true in meetings. Well-constructed meetings have topics related to student learning—instruction, curriculum, and assessment—that hold teacher interest and minimize the likelihood that teachers will avoid the work or engage in off-task behaviors.

Plan the Beginning

When planning the agenda, pay attention to flow, and plan in changes to the energy level from listening to talking, from larger group to small group work, from work to breaks, and so forth. Poorly constructed meetings are laden with announcements, reports, administrivia, and unclear outcomes. The beginning of the meeting is the most valuable instructional time and should be used wisely. Announcements should not be scheduled at the beginning of a meeting or at the end when people are packing to leave. Insert them somewhere in the middle as a transition from one agenda topic to another. The only reason announcements should be on a meeting agenda is if the item requires conversation to be implemented uniformly. The exception is details about the next meeting.

Cluster Reports

Reports sometimes dominate meeting time. Cluster reports together and assign them a tight time frame so those reporting have time only to provide the essence of their message and can follow up with written materials.

Mix Strategies

The effective facilitator makes sure to include a mix of strategies that support members working in pairs, trios, or in small groups, and sometimes working as a whole group to maintain members' interest. Group members will actively engage in well-constructed meetings.

2. Is Energy Waning?

Keep in mind that fatigue saps people's attention. As the group tires, members' auditory processes weaken, leading to a need to record more statements for the group or to use more strategies to involve the participants. Sometimes group members may need to stand and talk with someone not seated nearby just to get their energy back. Facilitators can have participants identify three or four different learning partners to meet with and engage with at strategic times—when the group needs to revitalize or when summary statements would be useful. Partners can be assigned by a season (winter, spring, etc.), by color, or by time of day.

When the group needs an energy break, the facilitator might say, "Meet with your 3 o'clock partner and anticipate parent response to this proposal."

Other energy-inducing strategies are listed here:

Around the Room and Back Again

- Write a prompt connected to something being studied, such as "ways to increase student time on task."
- Ask group members to think of one response to the prompt.
- Have participants move around the room and share responses without taking notes. Ask them to mentally catalog others' responses.
- Tell them that when their memory is full or at the signal, to return to their seats and list the responses they heard.
- Ask table groups to pool responses.
- Have the groups report, and if useful, record the responses on a chart that can be referred to during the ensuing conversation.

Card Partners

Use playing cards to form groups to keep energy high. The facilitator may need to shuffle or consciously arrange cards to break up cliques or table groups.

- Distribute a playing card to each individual (pick appropriate cards according to the size of the whole group and intended small groups) and have them meet according to one of the following patterns:

  ☐ Pair—same number, same color
  ☐ Pair—same number, different color

☐ Group of three—cards add up to 21 (same suit or different suit)

☐ Other combinations limited only by your imagination

The Card Stack and Shuffle

Engage people physically, visually, and cognitively by using index cards to capture and sort responses. Ask participants to do the following:

■ Complete two stems, such as "Good student writers . . ." and "Good teachers of writing . . ."
■ Write each response on a separate 3 × 5 card.
■ Stack and shuffle the cards at the table, then pass them to the table to the right.

The facilitator then models how to draw a card and explore the implications of one of the assumptions. The facilitator encourages paraphrasing and inquiry.

■ Select a card and read it to the table group.
■ Identify possible assumptions related to the response on the card.
■ Explore the implications of those assumptions.
■ Repeat the pattern, with other members of the table group drawing a card in turn.

3. Are Emotions Ratcheting Up?

Accomplished facilitators pay close attention to group and individual emotions. When emotions increase, facilitators need to be preemptive and attend to the shifts in energy. The higher the emotion, the more the facilitator will need to maintain tight structures and process frequently.

The less seasoned the group, the more members need tight structures in which they have few choices about how to participate. Less mature groups especially need to have the reasons and structures of a protocol explained. Tight protocols are also helpful for meetings covering hard-to-discuss or sensitive topics. Here are a few strategies should you anticipate high emotions.

First Turn/Last Turn

Have groups think about the topic that is subject to dispute. Sometimes a short reading or a quote can serve as a useful focus. When possible, have them read prior to the meeting. When at the meeting, organize into groups of four to six members. Instruct members to do the following:

- ☐ Individually review the text, and mark key ideas.
- ☐ The first person shares one of her marked items but does not comment on it.
- ☐ Group members comment on that first item with no crosstalk.
- ☐ Repeat the pattern around the table.

The facilitator monitors groups and intervenes when crosstalk occurs.

4. Might the Group Be Heading Toward Conflict?

Always adhere to the principle that when the group faces the potential for conflict, all voices need to be in the room for the topic to be addressed. Getting everyone who needs to be in the room to be present allows the facilitator the chance to explain the norm for respectful listening, to get everyone's voice in the room in a nonconfrontational manner, to allow people to connect with one another, to allow members to express hopes and apprehensions, to value thinking and feeling, and to elicit agendas that might not otherwise be heard.

Smart facilitators begin meetings in which they anticipate intrapersonal conflict by using grounding. The facilitator wants to honor cognitive conflict, which is needed for sound decisions, but to diminish affective conflict, and so preemptive strategies are invaluable. The grounding sets a tone, establishes respect for each voice, and provides members with safe ways to express themselves. The activity operates on earth time, not clock time, so the facilitator does not attempt to hurry a group along this important inclusion activity.

Grounding

- If the group is large, break members into groups of six to eight with a mechanism for reporting out at the end of the small group interactions.
- Explain that the purpose of the activity is to establish a norm for respectful listening.
- Explain the procedure, and post on a flip chart what members will talk about.

  - ☐ My name is . . .
  - ☐ My relationship to this topic is . . .
  - ☐ My expectations are . . .
  - ☐ How I feel about being here is . . .

- When members indicate that they understand the process, name the first speaker in each group, and have small group members then take turns speaking.
- Ask that when one member speaks, all others remain silent.

- Ask group members to give full nonverbal attention to the speaker.
- After everyone in the small group has spoken, have the first speaker summarize to the group what has been said.
- When all groups are finished, call on the first speaker in each group to give a summary statement to the full assembly.

Since the primary purpose of grounding is to give participants an opportunity to be heard, be sure members do not feel rushed. The harder the topic is to talk about, the more valuable the full-group grounding will be. With a group size of 40 to 50 people, this activity might take as long as an hour.

DECIDING WHEN TO INTERVENE

Roger Schwartz (2002) says that the decision to intervene is always contextual. His five most crucial considerations before intervening with the group are the following:

1. Is intervening important?
2. Am I the best person to intervene?
3. Are my observations accurate?
4. Will it be quick or take time?
5. Can the group learn from it?

1. Is Intervening Important?

Groups are fueled by intellectual and emotional energy, a common focus and process, transparent decision making, and fully disclosed information. Group member participation and consciousness about group work are components of this fuel.

Before intervening and affecting the group's energy, ask yourself if the behavior is significantly disruptive. Analyze possible immediate and long-term effects. Consider whether the behavior is disruptive enough to interfere with the group's work, how much the work is being hampered (whether it is delayed, slowed, or completely thrown off track) and whether the behavior will lead to other behaviors that will lessen the group's productivity as time goes on. Side talk, for example, often can be ignored if it is not affecting other group members' attentiveness.

Also consider the group's development. Can the group learn from the moment and become more aware of members' behaviors and choices, adding to the group's ability to self-monitor and self-correct?

2. Am I the Best Person to Intervene?

Sometimes a message from fellow group members can be more potent than a message from the facilitator. For example, in one group, a single member dominated airtime. Three colleagues became extremely annoyed and asked the facilitator to point out the behavior. In this case, the facilitator *could* take on the task of delivering the message, but it would be much more powerful coming from the three irritated members who owned the problem. The facilitator offered language to the three colleagues. They intervened and resolved the problem.

3. Are My Observations Accurate?

Our observations and interpretations can be wrong. Our perceptions are not trustworthy when we are tired or stressed. At these times, we are less likely to interpret objectively what is happening. The first maxim of facilitation should be, "Facilitator, take care of thyself." Make sure to rest and eat well. Arrange for a group break to regenerate if necessary.

4. Will It Be Quick, or Take Time?

Once a train has slowed, it requires extra energy to bring it back to speed. Once a group is idle, participants will begin off-topic conversations or mentally leave the room. The greater your repertoire of intervention strategies, the more extensive will be your choice of quick, one-stroke, brief corrections. The more credible the group finds you as a facilitator and the more mature as a group it is, the more permission you have to direct. Groups that have not reached a mature phase may require more explanations.

5. Can the Group Learn From It?

One way to extend a group's knowledge is by using a "process commercial," a brief statement of why you are using a particular intervention. To move beyond arguments about process, a facilitator might say, "There are no 'best' processes to prioritize, so instead of taking up time discussing the merits of different processes, let's just set this one in motion and see where we arrive."

SUMMARY

Gaining clarity about outcomes and deciding when to intervene are essential aspects of an accomplished facilitator's mindset. Clarity about outcomes—or intentions—is at the heart of any successful action plan. The confluence of intention and attention leads the facilitator to select behaviors most likely to achieve the meeting goals. Intentions drive attention. In this chapter, we emphasized clarity of outcome and explored preemptive interventions. As the facilitator begins to gauge when and how to intervene effectively and has a number of tools and strategies, the facilitator begins to demonstrate proficiency. The nuances of intervention are no longer a mystery, and more often than not are a discernible problem to solve. In the next chapter, we deal directly with the myriad of problems that come up in groups, from ambivalence to rudeness.

5

COMMON GROUP ISSUES

O nce the basics of proactive interventions are covered—setting the stage, creating an agenda, establishing standards, setting working agreements, and anticipating problems—facilitators can begin to develop strategies for more common group issues. What does the facilitator do when the basics are in place and the meeting still occasionally gets derailed? Facilitators must vigilantly monitor their response as well as group responses to the disruptive behaviors.

Facilitators should expect to run into roadblocks. We all have participated in meetings in which the group seems to go off track, attention wanes, group members talk over the facilitator, the discussion turns from the task to topics not relevant to the work, or workflow is otherwise hampered. In this chapter, we start with issues such as lack of attention, getting off track, resistant behavior, and other issues that can stymie groups. In some cases, we may repeat an intervention already described when it is the most efficient or best choice.

When dealing with distractions, a useful rule of thumb, when possible, is not to direct the group's focus to the distraction.

When we make the mistake of giving the distracting behavior our focus by putting a spotlight on it, we divert the group from the task. Even though an intervention is short, it breaks the group's focus on a topic. Brains that change focus do not easily return to center. Preferred strategies then call for the facilitator to maintain the group's focus on the topic while intervening with the disruption.

GETTING ATTENTION

In a workshop we attended, the facilitator was having a hard time getting the group's attention. Whenever he wanted members to pay attention to him, he signaled participants to look toward him and then started talking over the voices. While most groups do eventually quiet down, beginning to speak when the group is not quiet wastes valuable time and does not model a key component of listening—one voice in the room at a time.

One of the most striking differences between novice and accomplished facilitators is how they manage to help the group get on task and maintain or regain focus. To maintain attention, the facilitator must be congruent with the intended outcome. If, for example, the facilitator wants the group to be quiet, he models quietness. In addition, the facilitator is responsible for helping the group maintain focus. Effective facilitators monitor and adjust the group's work to keep group members' energy levels optimal and see to it that the group stays on target. The interventions listed here are listed from least intrusive to most intrusive.

Attention First

Both Grinder (1993) and Zoller (2010) strongly advocate that attention should always be the first order of business. Chapter 3 described standing in a credible stance and using a credible voice, one with a narrow range that drops at the end of sentences. To gain the group's attention, the facilitator will combine these features as follows:

- Assume a credible stance.
- Be still—as in freezing the posture.
- Announce in a credible voice, "Look this way please."
- Hold the posture and freeze a gesture until almost all the members are silent and focused.
- Conclude with "thank you" stated in a credible voice.
- When the group is attentive and still, break eye contact, breathe, and step into another space. Again, with a credible voice, give the next direction.

As groups tire, group members often respond less to verbal directions. During a working session, we often use a hand signal to redirect attention from small group conversation to full group work. Once again assume a credible stance, stand still, and now hold one hand in the air as a prearranged signal for silence. As group members notice the gesture, they copy it signaling to those who may not have noticed that you need their attention. The visual nature of this strategy gets attention from those who process visually, and their silence alerts auditory processers to pay attention (Garmston & Wellman, 2009, 2013).

Most often simple signals are enough to get attention. On the rare occasions when the group is engaged and side conversations are disturbing attention a facilitator might say, "I am sorry; we keep getting distracted because we have many conversations in the room (pause). We need to make sure everyone is ready to focus on the topic and have one conversation at a time." Or in more extreme situations, a facilitator might use the two-second complete message because it is brief and contains data, a feeling state and a direction such as: "I am having trouble hearing (data). I feel frustrated when some are not able to participate because their comments are being overridden (feeling). We need to have one voice in the room at a time (direction)."

As with all direct messages, the facilitator's tone of voice needs to be neutral and direct and include the credible drop at the end. We suggest practicing in advance.

REFOCUSING

At one time or another, most groups will be loud and either off track or so heavily engaged in the work they are oblivious to directions. Either way, the facilitator's role is to stick to the agenda and help the group accomplish its goals. Doing so requires that the facilitator have members' attention, which is not always the case. Skilled facilitators have several methods for quieting the group when members are talking and it is time to move ahead.

Common Signal

- Model attention and listening: As described earlier under Attention First, pause and freeze. Stand with your hand raised in a visible location, eyes lowered, and wait for silence. When 90% of group members are paying attention, say, "Thank you," in a credible voice.
- When all eyes are on you, pause, breathe, step to a new location, and give directions.
- When the group is large, consider pairing a sound or light signal with the nonverbal signal.

■ Asking all participants to also raise a hand when they hear the signal helps all those in the room recognize that the facilitator is giving the signal for change. The most visually oriented people will respond first to the signal. The auditory people will then hear the volume shift and also be quiet.

Physical Proximity

Just like the skilled teacher, the skilled facilitator is continually conscious of group behaviors. The skilled teacher knows that when a few students are talking, moving closer to them while continuing to teach often can quiet the conversation. Teachers call this intervention *proximity.*

When most group members' eyes follow the facilitator, the speakers will notice that everyone is paying attention and will re-engage. This subtle psychological phenomenon reminds us that humans are social animals. Without realizing it, we more often than not mirror the behavior of those around us.

The facilitator's role is to keep attention where it needs to be so that the group can reach its goals.

Verbal Proximity

If it seems awkward or impossible to move closer to the speakers, try using verbal proximity.

Cup a hand to your ear, lean sideways toward the competing voices, maintain eye contact with the group rather than the speakers, and say, "I am sorry I cannot hear you, (name). Please wait."

Another option is to make a general comment, such as, "When several conversations are occurring at the same time, it is difficult for everyone to hear. Let's hold on until everyone is listening."

Continue speaking only after all are quiet. If someone else in the group was being interrupted, wait for quiet and say, "Go ahead and finish what you had to say."

REDIRECTING ENGAGEMENT

Groups often require redirection both to ensure participants remain engaged and to help the group remain efficient and effective in its work. While members sometimes seem not to be engaged, their behaviors often have more to do with the facilitator's failure to give clear directions or read group members' underlying motivations and intentions. Some common behaviors and redirection strategies follow.

Join a Whole Table That Is Off Task

If a group is off task, try joining the group to establish rapport and interact quietly. Often your presence is enough to get them back on track, or at other times, you'll learn that they were confused and you can assist by clarifying directions. If subgroups are working and a table is off task, there are several strategies to try.

- Use increasing proximity. Move closer, and closer, and then listen in by getting down and directing an ear, not your eyes toward the group.
- If proximity alone does not help the group redirect, assume positive intentions and say, "It appears that my directions did not help you get started. What can I do to help you now?"
- Elicit participants' help, saying, "Help me understand where you are in the process."

- Restate the rationale for the activity and describe what value it has to the group. For example, say, "This work is important for us in that it . . . What is the first step you need to take?"

- Notice whether the behavior is centered on process objections, and offer an alternative task. Say, "I notice that you do not seem to want to do this work in this way. Is there another way to accomplish this task? Perhaps you should break up the task and regroup into pairs."

Refocus Serial Storytelling

Serial storytelling can take many forms. Sometimes groups are pining for the "good old days." Other times, they may feel threatened and are protecting the status quo. In some groups, a few participants tend to dominate with their stories. Varying tactics can help redirect the group or person to the task at hand. When other strategies discussed earlier are not effective, try more direct options.

- Call attention to the storytelling as an abstraction: "While these stories are interesting, hearing them may take more time than we have. The data we need are often embedded in the story. In the interest of time, when it is your turn to share, please report the point you wish to make without telling the story."

- Report observable data: "You may have noticed that the last three comments have slipped into storytelling. This will slow us down or may distract from the task."

- Inquire: "What is happening right now with the storytelling, and how is this affecting the group's progress?"

- Use the behavior as a teachable moment: "Notice how we have slipped into lengthy storytelling. What would you do if you were facilitating?"

WHEN WORKFLOW IS HAMPERED

A high school in Los Angeles has adopted departmental and cross-disciplinary professional learning teams to address their work with EL students. Several groups struggled in the beginning with a few members who were so focused on process to the exclusion of getting work done that the sessions wound up in process fights. Keep in mind that the purpose of groups is to get work done, and when interferences occur, the facilitator's job is to get the group back on task.

Address a Refusal to Follow Directions

The facilitator of a high school faculty session wanted the group to process data that had been collected from sensing interviews. She asked faculty members to divide into groups and was surprised by a teacher who stood up and said, "We don't want to break into groups. We want to talk about this all together."

Veteran facilitators know to avoid lengthy arguments about process. The facilitator might have been taken aback or flustered, but experiences provided her with several strategies that she could quickly call on to smooth the situation and keep the group on course, including the following.

- Apologize for not stating the rationale for the process and then explaining the steps in the planned process. For example, for breaking into smaller groups, explain that the goal is to gain greater participation by more people, followed by a full group conversation.

- Reply that the naysayer's idea is another way to approach the matter at hand. Ask the group to get a sense of the most useful approach by pairing off to talk about the pros and cons of this suggestion. Be clear in advance that when the group's preferences are split, the facilitator chooses.
- Continue with the suggested course of action saying that many processes would help us get the job done, but having started down this path, let's continue and save time by not changing processes.
- Provide more structure by charting some prompts to guide the conversation: "What surprises do you see in the data?" "What patterns do you see?" "What assumptions do you make about causes?"

Assist With Difficulty Transitioning

When the group has difficulty transferring attention to the next agenda item, the facilitator's role is to help members understand the challenge. The facilitator may try the following:

- Try to be flexible about time. Assess the value of the discussion compared with the agenda items. Point out to the group that the discussion is taking longer than anticipated or planned. Add time.
- Give the group a two-minute warning or some other transition signal to prepare to change direction.
- Acknowledge at the beginning of the session that time will be a factor and that the group may not get to discuss some issues. Clarify that the goal is to engage, not complete.
- Acknowledge that leaving a good discussion is difficult, and ask the group to decide how to proceed or to set up another time to finish the agenda.

Address Uneven Finishes With Group Work

When different group members or small groups work on the same task, they seldom finish at exactly the same time. The challenge for the facilitator is to help the whole group remain engaged and to encourage those who are taking longer to finish the work.

Ask members to hold up fingers representing the additional time they need. Give them a range such as two to four minutes. Say aloud the number of fingers you see in each request, and then announce you are allocating more time, an average of what you have seen. Because you verbalize the variation in requests, members accept that subgroups are in different stages of completion. This alerts all the group's members that different people need different amounts of time for the task and encourages the faster processing people to be patient while the others complete the work. It also serves to speed up slower groups.

Energize a Quiet Group

Groups have their own energy levels. Some groups are high energy and talkative. Others seem to have lower energy and are quiet, sometimes seeming shy or afraid to talk. Occasionally, you have members who hesitate to comment or ask questions. When the group is so quiet that discussion is lagging, facilitators can help.

- Think-ink-share. Give members time to jot some notes and then initiate a round-robin response in which each person in a small group makes a comment about the topic.
- Have the group divide into pairs to work. Invite partners to report what their colleagues said.
- Change the energy in the room by mixing up participants. Simply say, "Stand up and find a new partner whom you

have not talked with today." Or assign random groupings using lineups: "Line up in alphabetical order related to the profession you might have chosen had you not entered education." Regroup based on the random order provided by the lineup.

Once, in Singapore, Bob worked with a group that he knew was full of participants who would hesitate to be the first to speak. He began the sessions by offering a rationale for group participation and outlining the positive effects of group work. He offered the group information about working smarter and told members what to expect from his facilitation.

At the beginning of the session he said, "When I ask group members to report out, I will randomly choose who will summarize the group view, so you will want to listen carefully. In small groups talk about . . . and be ready to report back when I give this signal."

When it was time to report out, Bob used various descriptors to identify who was asked to speak:

- "This time, the person with the most elaborate shoes will report."
- "The person who traveled farthest to get here this morning will report."
- "The group member who woke earliest this morning gets to report."

MANAGING YOUR EMOTIONS

Finally, any of the previous situations, perhaps exacerbated by fatigue, inadequate time, or unrelated personal concerns, can conspire to get you emotionally off balance. When you find you are becoming emotionally hooked, it is useful to deal directly with the behavior and to honestly convey how the behavior affects your emotional state. First, and always, move to a new space and take a deep cleansing breath before speaking. This is a breath from deep in the diaphragm, sometimes called a belly breath in which your abdomen expands on the inhale. Then authentically pair an "I feel" message with an "I think" statement about the group's needs.

- Signal a change in the agenda: "Let's take time out to review our agreements."
- State observable data: "Today there are many side conversations."
- Give personal feelings. "When this happens I start to get confused and lose track of what is being said."
- State the impact on the group: "I think this may also be confusing to some who are listening."
- State the need: "Both for respect and efficiency, the agreement about one conversation at a time needs to be kept."
- Signal a change back to the meeting. "(Name) has the floor, and then after that (name) has her hand up. After that, we'll see who else wants to talk."

POSITIONAL THINKING—POWER STRUGGLES

We tend to approach issues from our own viewpoint and needs. Without realizing it, most of us adopt positions that frame our needs or wants. When these positions are in conflict, groups get into power struggles. When the issues are not so important to us, we often reach consensus; however, when the issues are important and life changing such as those found in collective bargaining, we find ourselves in conflict. Those trained in interest-based bargaining (IBB) have learned how to help groups identify interests as criteria for sorting options and positions. Identifying interests means that we go behind our positions and ask why until we come up with multiple interests. For example, a common position, albeit often unstated, is "I have invested hours and hours into my curriculum, and I am, thus, resistant to changes." In this example, the primary interest is stated: time efficiency. However, with further exploration, one might also discover that other interests about change are that new curriculum (1) adds value to current lesson planning, (2) is easy to learn, and (3) has processes that can overlay on current practices. John Glaser (2005), an expert in IBB, suggests that the necessary reframe is from "imposing favorite solutions" to "authentically engaging in a joint search for solutions" (p. 109). By seeking out interests, groups can find points of coherence, places where their interests intersect. Glaser advises that this concept is easily understood, but the ability to hear and apply interests is subtle and takes much practice.

From Positions to Interests: Basic Interest-Based Bargaining Step

- Invite the group to shift gears and assume an inquiry stance to seek out the reasons behind some of our strongly held beliefs and positions.
- Remind the group that this requires that we suspend judgment for the period of inquiry.
- Create a T-chart with opposing positions stated at the top of each column, such as "in school suspension" versus "out of school suspension."
- List the interests, the reasons why that solution is in the groups' best interest.

- Ask the group to test their interests against these criteria listed on a posted chart:

  □ Interests

    - Are satisfied in multiple ways
    - Sound like motivations
    - Answer the question, "Why is it important to . . . ?"
    - Are criteria against which to measure a position

- Keep the chart and use it as a set of criteria for evaluating the different positions.

When groups have not had much practice in this kind of thinking, positions will creep onto the chart. With novices, the intervention works best if the facilitator tests each statement with the criteria before writing it down. As groups progress, several participants will begin to help others reframe their positions. Finding interests is not always easy for those who are decisive and know what they want!

SUMMARY

Some challenges are fairly common to groups yet become quite manageable for the developing facilitator. Strategies for getting attention, refocusing groups, redirecting to task, and managing interruptions in workflow are described in this chapter. When facilitators take care of themselves, as described in Chapters 1 and 2, and hold positive presuppositions about members' intentions, they are less likely to become emotionally activated by group behavior. Facilitators learn how to manage these issues by tackling one problem at a time and rehearsing and practicing facilitation moves that reinforce principles, norms, and working agreements. Over time, these interventions should become routine. Help groups identify interests and how they might be satisfied when power struggles emerge. Alternately, help groups seek the truth that exists in the opposing views. In the next chapter, we will cover issues with specific personality habits that show up in meetings, such as the "silent one" or the "long-winded one."

6

MANAGING COMMON CHALLENGES

F acilitators continue to struggle with several common problems that interrupt workflow. The stresses in the 21st-
century workplace have increased exponentially, and smart
people can deviate from norms of civility. Rock (2009) describes
how workers "are experiencing an epidemic of overwhelm" (p. 4).
In business, health care, or schools, demands are constant and over-
whelming, leaving many fatigued and less resourceful. Workers'
fatigue is compounded by seemingly never-ending requirements for
higher performance, greater productivity, and countless demands
for accountability. As a result, groups are experiencing diminished
capacity to process information and stay focused. Rock reminds us
that the brain is exquisitely powerful, yet there are biological limits
to our mental performance, and that groups under stress reach these
limits sooner rather than later.

This chapter offers responses to several manifestations of
workplace stress that take two major forms, either low engagement
or disruptive behavior. We've used verbs as shorthand to describe

people exhibiting problematic behaviors but are clear that no one is their behavior at any given moment. We are all complex and well-intentioned beings, and we sometimes make less-than-desirable choices. In the category of low engagement, we describe the knitter (leave them alone), the daydreamer, and the distracted. Among the disruptive behaviors, we give suggestions for addressing the long-winded, the resister, the know-it-all, and the interrupter. The intervention strategies are presented with the safest responses listed first.

LOW ENGAGEMENT

Group facilitators report to us that lack of engagement is their primary challenge. Sometimes, as we describe in Chapter 4, group participation is affected when participants aren't adhering to working agreements, such as agreeing not to use cell phones. In more challenging situations, participants are initially engaged and then withdraw. The skilled facilitator must decide whether and how to work with the group member to get the group back on track. Preemptively, when you want participants to be engaged, you plan structures that invite their active participation.

Knitters

This person brings quiet, nondisruptive work that may not require their full attention. For some, doing handwork helps them listen. We recommend the facilitator do the following:

- Leave the person alone.
- Offer a short commercial about respecting cognitive styles if the knitting becomes an issue with others.

Nonparticipants

Often, one group member will be reluctant to take part in the group's activities. The person's reluctance may stem from a range of causes, from personality to personal issues—he may be having an off day. The facilitator's job is to be sure the group works at maximum capacity. The facilitator may try the following:

- State an abstraction:

  "It is going to be important to have every voice in the room as this is an important issue."

- Change the group structure by using one of the following statements:

  "Get up and find someone you have not talked to today, and . . .

  - ☐ summarize what we have discussed."
  - ☐ identify the most important points."
  - ☐ generate any unanswered questions."
  - ☐ check in to verify for yourself that topic has been covered and the group is ready to move on."

- Give directions to change seating to create random partnerships. For example, try the following:

  - ☐ Lineups. Say, "Place yourself in a line by birthday, beginning with those born in January over here and those in December over here."
  - ☐ Numbering off.
  - ☐ Dealing out matched pairs from a deck of cards and having members pair off.

- ▪ Name a behavior: "I notice that some participants have not spoken up."
- ▪ Inquire: "Can we hear from someone who hasn't had a chance to talk yet?"
- ▪ Inquire specifically: "Charise, you served on a similar committee last year. Is there anything you'd like to add?"

Daydreamers

This is a person who is giving less than full attention to the group by fidgeting, dozing, appearing distracted, or dividing attention with another full cognitive task, such as reading unrelated text. The accomplished facilitator pays attention to the ebb and flow of the group's energy and plans changes that affect energy levels to help sustain the group throughout the course of the meeting. To keep energy high or renew spirits, try the following:

- ▪ Change interaction to more active stance:
  - ☐ Switch the group from listening to talking, either as a whole group or in partners or trios.
  - ☐ Shift the meeting focus. Ask, "Given these facts, what actions might you take?"
  - ☐ Shift from the abstract to the concrete: "What seems to be the big idea here?"
  - ☐ Check in with the group: "What questions do you have?" Or, "Is anything still unclear?"
  - ☐ Summarize: "Let's summarize what the group thinks they need to remember."
- ▪ Change positions. Get participants to stand up:
  - ☐ Give the direction: "Stand up, find someone not at your table; check in with them about what they are thinking

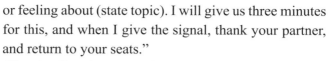

or feeling about (state topic). I will give us three minutes for this, and when I give the signal, thank your partner, and return to your seats."

☐ Give the direction: "For the next set, to get new energy in the room, we are going to switch groups. Pack up your belongings, get up, and find three people you have not talked with yet today."

■ Use a refocusing move.

☐ Stop, take a breath, and move toward a visual third point of reference, either a posted agenda, or hold up the paper agenda and point at the agenda item, say, "Right now, we are focusing on . . ." (See Third Point in Chapter 7.)

☐ Stop, take a breath, and move your position slightly. Hold up the number of fingers you need to review key points. Say, "We have just covered *two* important points. Point 1 (with one finger up) is _____, and Point 2 (with two fingers up) is _____."

Silent Participants

Some group members are naturally more reticent. The skilled facilitator involves all group members to maximize the group's potential to accomplish the best work. Involving silent members is important, but how that is accomplished is even more important.

■ Use pair-share more often. Once someone has spoken up in a small group, they are more likely to speak up in a larger group.

■ Ask for reports of "what your partner said." This guarantees that the quiet voice comes into the room.

- Contract outside the meeting for a quiet person who knows a lot about a particular subject to have a specific presentation at the meeting.
- Ask for comments from those who have not yet spoken.
- Use hand signals to find degrees of agreement. "If you are in agreement give a thumbs up, if you are not sure or could go either way, show a thumbs sideways, and if you disagree, show a thumbs down." This respects a quiet person's desire to remain quiet, and also helps you know where they stand on an issue.

Frowners

We know that most of our communication is nonverbal. The facilitator may notice the person who sits frowning with arms crossed, slumping in the chair, and instinctively assume that this is negativity directed either at the topic or the group. Rarely is this true. Humans are wired to presume the negative—it has been an asset to our survival. But more often than not, the person either is in a deep thinking posture or is distracted by a personal agenda that is causing distress. Presume the person is taking care of himself in some way. The facilitator may try the following:

- At a break time or when small groups are talking, get on eye level with the participant and offer data and then a question: "I noticed your eyebrows were scrunched, and I wondered if you are okay. Are you all right?" We've learned that we will hear one of four types of responses:

  ☐ I'm not feeling well (physical).
  ☐ I don't know if my teenage son found the car keys this morning to get to school (personal emotional).

- ☐ I had to suspend a kid yesterday, and I can't get it off my mind (work emotional).
- ☐ I disagree with what is going on (present situation).

When the present situation is causing the person distress, ask, "Can you tell me what parts of today you disagree with?" The principles at work here are observe carefully and describe behaviorally, without judgmental words ("you looked upset") and listen deeply, being prepared to respectfully interact with the person's area of disagreement.

Distracteds

Occasionally a person's attention is diverted elsewhere: grading papers, scoring tests, working on calendars, or accessing information on the Internet. The facilitator may try the following:

- Restructure work using any of the regrouping ideas offered in the examples previously, including structuring movement in the room. Changing physiology often changes a person's internal state, and he is more likely to return to a seat ready to participate.
- Use a variation of pair-share, asking partners to report the other person's idea. In one version, mix-freeze-pair, participants mill about the room and at a signal, talk with the nearest person.
- Ask if the person would like to add a comment at an appropriate time, framing the question so that the person can say no without being embarrassed.
- Invite the person up to record or perform some other service to the group.

■ Let the group decide if they need to adopt a working agreement. When Diane was a principal, one staff decided that they would be allowed to bring in other work (not all parts of a meeting are pertinent to all), however, when Diane needed their undivided attention she would signal this. Sometimes Diane wrote it right on the agenda: "Today we are going to make many decisions about how to handle parent conferences. I want everyone's thinking in the room. Leave your distractions in your classroom. Thank you." Other times she simply signaled a transition at the meeting by saying something like, "This is the part of the meeting where your undivided attention is needed. If you have a distraction out, it is time to put it away."

DISRUPTIVE GROUP MEMBERS

Disruptive group members often do not want to disturb the order, but they respond out of passion, frustration, or anger and are unaware of their impact on the group. They disrupt perhaps because they think others are not listening, are angry because time has been wasted, or sometimes are just bored. When participants vehemently agree or disagree with a point, the intensity of their energy becomes the distraction. Some general strategies can help keep groups working effectively. To raise consciousness and increase the options for responsible participation, try these steps:

■ Organize the talking. "Whoops! Hang on. There are several conversations going on right now. Many people want to comment. Let's line them up. Daphine, you're first; John will be second; Kenya will follow John; then Carlotta is number four, and Saundra is five. Remember your numbers. Okay, Daphine, start us off."

▦ Describe the behavior and ask for a summary. "There are only three people talking right now and everyone else is watching. Can those of you who have been listening describe the various viewpoints?" (Note: This can also be done in a pair share and then reported.)

▦ Stop the discussion. Say, "Hold on, I need to check in with the group. It seems people are repeating themselves. Does the group need any more information? Is the group ready to make a decision? Let's hear some brief advocacies for the various options. One idea at a time. You can advocate as often as you like as long as the advocacies are brief and stated in the positive. No speeches, please."

▦ Agree to disagree. "It seems you are not going to get agreement today. Let's summarize what you've agreed on, and what has not yet been resolved. Can you live with this for now and agree to disagree agreeably on what has not been settled until we address this again?"

▦ Ask questions. "How is the group doing on its norm of listening to one another? Tell your partner and then let's hear some reports." "What's going on right now?" "Talk to a trio. Is there an elephant in the room that is not being talked about? Decide how we might bring up some of these tough issues."

For particular types of disruptive behavior, try the suggestions listed next. Some facilitators, when adding new strategies to their repertoire, make note cards for specific situations and refer to these discretely during a meeting.

Broken Records

This person continues to repeat the same concept or idea and can't be dissuaded from speaking repeatedly. To intervene, the facilitator may try the following:

- Restructure and break the pattern of full group participation by asking the group to form pairs, trios, or small groups.
- Paraphrase, chart the comment, then give the point emphasis by circling the comment and asking, "Is this what you want the group to know?"
- If the comment is made again, go to the chart, underline what you previously recorded, and say, "This is what you want the group to know."
- Paraphrase or ask the group to paraphrase. This lets the speaker know she has been heard. "Turn to a partner and summarize the key point you think Samuel has made about _____."
- Acknowledge the behavior, "I notice some voices have been silent. Turn to your partner and check to see if there is anything else we need to know about _____."
- Employ satisfy, satisfy, delay. Respond with a comment or a paraphrase if the person persists. Next time, satisfy again with a comment or paraphrase. On the third exchange, briefly acknowledge and then turn to the rest of the room and say, "We need to hear from others in the room." Or pose a question for small groups to consider, breaking the interactive pattern.

Long-Winded Speakers

Some people are naturally long-winded. Their verbosity is a manifestation of a cognitive style, and often the talkers are unaware of how the lengthiness of their comments affects the group. Unfortunately, these people can monopolize meeting time and turn off other meeting participants. To facilitate a meeting with long-winded people, remember that a general rule for any intervention is to start with the most subtle or mild redirect cues, and then increase the strength of the intervention as needed.

- When the speaker is catching his or her breath, say something like, "Mary, thank you for your ideas (redirect). Brent, do you have any comments about (paraphrase Mary's idea)?"

- Try a nonverbal stop sign. A common sign is to hold up a hand, palm outward, toward the speaker. The speaker will receive this better if you accompany the action with a neutral face and an invitation to "Hold on. Let's give others a chance to talk." Don't thrust your hand out too quickly—that can be perceived as an aggressive act.

- Another nonverbal tactic is the "A-ha sign." The sign is one finger held up and signifies that you are enthusiastic about the speaker's point. Generally, follow this sign with a comment such as, "Jay, your point about (topic) is important to you. Let's hear what Shannon thinks about that idea. She looks like she wants to speak."

- Finally, you may have to take a strong stance. For example, interrupt the speaker with, "Fred, the group agreed that it is important that we accomplish x, y, and z before we leave today. I appreciate your comments, but we need to move on. Perhaps if there is time at the end of the meeting, we can come back to this." Then move immediately to the next agenda item. Keep in mind that this approach may result in some ruffled feathers. It may be appropriate to speak privately to the long-winded person after the meeting to explain why you felt this intervention was necessary to accomplish the meeting goals.

Humorists

Laughter can be a cue that people are nervous and need comic relief. The facilitator must discern if the comedic comments are helpful or are distracting the group from accomplishing its purpose. Sarcasm can get laughter as well, yet can be hurtful. If this is the case, see the *inappropriate humorist.* When faced with funny comments the facilitator can try the following:

- Join the group in laughter and when the laughter subsides, move on. While finishing up your laugh say, "That was funny! Let's refocus on _____."

  As the laughter subsides, redirect the group by moving to third point (see Chapter 7), and reinforcing the shift with a verbal cue, such as, "We are moving to _____."

- Find something in the comment that is close to a serious answer, and repeat the rephrased comment in a serious tone to the group. "Yes, that group of parents can truly be challenging. However, we need to focus on what is within our control."
- Confront the sarcasm directly: "That felt like a put-down. One principle for effective group work is that we go soft on people, but hard on ideas. The idea that needs attention now is_____."

Inappropriate Humorists

Like misinformation, inappropriate humor can poison the group's thinking. At a minimum, it will distract group members. It is important not to let inappropriate humor go by; the more inappropriate, the more important it is for the facilitator to break role and intervene with content. Some facilitator options are here:

- If you think the humorous comment is inappropriate but not offensive to group members, refrain from laughing, break eye contact, and then listen for an opening in the laughter to shift your posture and redirect the group's attention back to the topic at hand, saying, "Our focus needs to be on _____."
- If you think the comment is offensive, signal a change in your role by moving to a new spot away from where you were facilitating and assume a voice of authority. In a credible voice (see *Congruence* in Chapter 3), make one of the following statements:

  - □ "While that remark was probably not intended to cause discomfort, this is a pretty sensitive topic, and that kind of humor makes some people uncomfortable. The group needs to focus on _____."
  - □ "Personally, I don't find that remark very funny. You may not be aware that some people might find that remark offensive. We need to move on."
  - □ "Comments that put a person or group down or demean them in some way take away from a group's ability to work together. We need to move on."

Latecomers and Early Leavers

Those who come in late or leave early can drain energy from the group. To intervene effectively, it's essential to remain neutral to the behavior and never to put the group or its members in the position of being wrong. (See Chapter 3 on working agreements.) To work with this behavior, the skilled facilitator can try the following:

- Always start on time, and engage the group right away with something that is light, relevant, and useful. Have table groups review the group's working agreements to select several to focus on during the current meeting. Those who are just a few minutes late can fold into the activity unobtrusively.

- Start with paired verbal fluency in which pairs designate an A and B partner. Each will take turns responding to a prompt. The prompt might be "everything you remember from the last meeting." Partner A speaks for 60 seconds, then Partner B for the same amount of time without repeating anything Partner A said. Partner A speaks again for 45 seconds, then Partner B. If you hold a third round, run it for 30 seconds or slightly less.

- On occasions in which there are not enough people in the room to begin the meeting, announce a new start time, and offer a generous interpretation, such as people may be held up in traffic.

- Assign a greeter to manage latecomers by greeting them as they enter and orienting them to what the group is doing.

- Acknowledge the newcomer's presence by briefly greeting the person. For example, say, "Hi, George. The group is working on _____ today," and then continue the interaction with the group.

- When several members are persistently late, acknowledge the situation without assigning blame and ask the group to help solve the problem. Have the group list strategies they use to make sure they are on time. Set a goal that everyone will be on time at the next meeting.

▪ Move introductions to the end of the meeting. It makes it harder for folks to walk out, and often, people remember each other better after having had some interaction. Point out that introductions were delayed by saying something like, "We've been working hard all day in this room and haven't done introductions yet. Because it's important to all of us to learn who is here, please stand and say your name."

▪ Announce critical information just after a break rather than at the beginning or end of a meeting so that everyone is present to hear it.

▪ If the situation involves just one individual who is perpetually late, invite the person to a private meeting:

☐ "Can you stop by after school today? I'd like to talk about the meeting and the group's working agreements."

☐ To give the person time to reflect, insist on meeting a bit later in the day. Many will come already willing to talk about making change.

☐ Establish a positive tone: "Thanks for stopping by. What I want to talk to you about is important."

☐ State observable data: "You were 10 minutes late to the meeting. Several other days you've arrived late." State thoughts or feelings: "I feel concerned for the group when you are not aligned with the working agreements."

☐ Ask, "What seems to be the problem?" Then listen empathetically.

☐ Express a need as an implied direction: "The group needs to know that you will be on time to the next meeting. What can you do to assure that this will happen?" If the person interrupts, ask them to let you give the entire message and say that you then will give them time to comment. The purpose of the *complete message* (see Chapter 4) is to avoid excuses or blame, and instead provide observable data, the resultant impact, and the need for a change.

☐ Wait for a response. Most people will respond right away. If they do not and the silence becomes uncomfortable, it is appropriate to state again, in a neutral tone, "I need to hear your perspective," followed by silence. Silence also communicates, "I am giving you my full attention, and I am ready to listen," a nondefensive and respectful stance from a facilitator.

Resisters

Sometimes, facilitators face a group of people who may not be interested in being present but are required to be there. Use structures that invite positive intentions or strategies to help members become conscious of their moods and the choices they have about these moods. Facilitators can try the following:

- Make meetings more engaging and renewing by having a time for socializing and a time for working.
- To increase buy in, have small groups help build the agendas, and try to get at least one of the more negative participants into the planning phase.
- REM. Introduce the session with an invitation to be responsible for one's own comfort and learning. Try saying, "To begin, I want to introduce you to REM, not the rapid eye movements of sleep, but a tip for you all to get the most value out of today.

First, don't sleep. The 'R' stands for 'responsible'—for your own comfort and learning. Move when you have to and monitor your need for liquid intake and output. Speak up when you cannot hear. The 'E' stands for 'experimentation.' Feel free to experiment with new ways of looking at things. The 'M,' for those of you who were mandated to be here, stands for misery, which, of course, is optional."

- Best/worst. Change expectations by saying, early in the meeting, "Turn to a partner and share the worst thing that could happen in the meeting today." After each person has shared, ask the pairs to share the best thing that could happen today. Record the ideas. Make an agreement that if any of the worst things happen, members will make a collective groan. This establishes a sense of group control over the events of the session and releases emotional tension.

- Pace and lead. Make a statement that parallels the participants' possible experience and then focuses them on the work of the day, "I can imagine that this is a topic that makes some of you cringe because _____. Today we are focusing on _____. My hope for today is _____." (See *Pace and Lead* in Chapter 7.)

- Banned words. Acknowledge the feeling in the room and say, "Sometimes to get things done, groups have to revisit overworked topics. Which words would you like not to hear today?" Make a list of banned words and then say, "I propose we all groan loudly if I or any group member uses any of these words." Rehearsing usually gets a laugh.

- Dump and jump: Invite participants to reflect on the day and then to move into the meeting. Allowing a brief reflection helps participants shift their thinking from busy

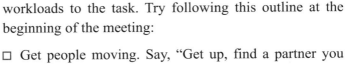

workloads to the task. Try following this outline at the beginning of the meeting:

- ☐ Get people moving. Say, "Get up, find a partner you have not talked to today, and in your pair assign yourselves the letter A or B."
- ☐ Check with the group: "Everyone should be in a pair and have a letter assigned. Raise your hand if you do not have a letter." Create a group of three if necessary.
- ☐ Use lights or a sound to give the group a signal after offering this direction: "When I give the signal, those who are letter A will have 90 seconds to share everything on your minds right now. When I give the signal again, Bs will have 90 seconds to share."
- ☐ After both 90-second cycles, stop the group and say, "Now for the final round, each of you have a minute to answer the question, What do you most want to get out of our meeting today? Start with Partner B, and then when I give the signal, Partner A gets a turn. When I give the final signal, thank your partner, and sit down."

Side Talkers

Side talk is the most common distraction facilitators report to us. These sidebars can lead to greater problems if not dealt with proactively. Skilled facilitators master a few simple ways of redirecting energy. The facilitator can try the following:

- ▦ Do not speak until all is quiet. Even skilled facilitators often miss this amazingly simple structure. Skilled facilitators have learned to give a signal and then quietly wait for attention rather than speaking over other voices. For example, with a raised hand (see *Attention First* in

Chapter 5) say, "Everyone focus here please," and then wait for full attention. Quiet begets quiet.

■ Use physical proximity to quiet the disrupters by moving closer and closer to the offenders while maintaining eye contact with the group member who currently is speaking. Proximity will often quiet down a group. If not, interject a comment such as the following:

- ☐ "Hang on a minute. I'm having trouble hearing because there is more than one voice in the room."
- ☐ "When multiple conversations are occurring at the same time, it is hard for the group to maintain focus."
- ☐ "Oh, did you want to say something? Please tell the group."
- ☐ "How does the group feel about the level of attentiveness right now?"
- ☐ Say to distracted leaders who are talking off task, "Can I ask you to quietly step out of the room to finish your conversation? When you are ready to come back, I'll help orient you so you can reengage."

Know-It-Alls

The know-it-all's underlying motive may be gaining recognition for her knowledge and contribution. Ironically, the more know-it-alls talk, the less likely the group is to give them the acknowledgment they so crave. Participants who feel listened to most often do not feel the need to repeat ideas. When group members talk over others, facilitators can try the following:

■ Judiciously use paraphrasing. Paraphrasing is the quickest and most neutral intervention. A paraphrase summarizes and makes the message succinct while communicating listening and understanding.

- Ask for clarification: "Can you tell us a bit more about (pick one narrow point)?"
- Invite specific evidence: "Can you give us a brief example of when that happened to you?"
- Validate the person: "This seems important. Can you state the key points again so that we can keep them in mind?"
- When comments are in conflict with what others in the group are saying, say to the group, "Turn to a partner and summarize the two points of view that are in the room."
- After a brief time, ask, "What questions does anyone have about the different points of view?"
- Monitor comments to be sure that ideas that are repeated do not give one viewpoint more weight.
- Move on as quickly as is feasible toward the productive work at hand.

Monopolizers

Like the know-it-all, these people often feel unheard. They can dominate a discussion. Sometimes, they are aware of their behavior and might even begin their comments with, "I don't mean to get on my soapbox, but _____." Skilled facilitators can use paraphrasing to help them know their messages have been heard and registered. Succinctly paraphrase their position, and then comment, "Let's hear what the rest of the group has to say. Who else has a comment on this topic?"

That may not be enough to stop a dedicated monopolizer. Follow up by trying the following:

- Succinctly paraphrase again. Then state, "It is important that we have a chance to hear from a number of people." Call on a new speaker.

■ Next, ask the group to reestablish the working agreement: "We agreed that we wanted all voices in the room, let's hear from someone who has not yet spoken. What else are we thinking?"

■ Explain, "I appreciate your comments, and it is important for everyone to have a chance to talk."

■ Wait for a breath, and interrupt by asking another person to comment: "(Name), can you tell us what you are thinking?"

The Rhetorician

Often a student or teacher of rhetoric, this person sees conversations as opportunities to argue and enjoy debate. This person will dominate groups with oratory, causing many members to participate less. Over time, this can disillusion the group and render work ineffective. Approaches vary acknowledging and using this person's skill to inform the group, to helping the group learn to dialogue on some topics and eliminate that rhetoric.

■ Use concise paraphrases to capture a key idea and chart it, thus, slowing the flow of ideas and having them stand still for examination by others.

■ Lead a conversation, one point at a time from the charted material. Insist that others speak before the rhetorician has another turn.

■ If appropriate, ask the rhetorician to reveal his thinking—the forms of logic he is employing as identification for the group.

■ Have people privately assess the meeting, focusing on the standard of balanced participation. At the next meeting, make whatever dissatisfactions with participation balance known to the group. Inquire about solutions.

▪ Bring to the group's attention that a member frequently uses rhetoric to approach topics and that this is a valuable skill, yet time consuming. Disclose the distinctions between rhetoric and dialogue (Garmston & Wellman, 2009, 2013), and suggest the group adopt one approach or the other depending on the outcome. Stress that rhetoric is used to win arguments while dialogue is to gain understanding of topics. Based on this awareness, consider the following approaches.

☐ Create a chart listing on one side the attributes of rhetoric and on the other the attributes of dialogue. (See Garmston with von Frank [2012] for distinguishing discussion and dialogue.) Having distinguished between the two, get agreement from the group about which form should apply to which agenda topics.

☐ List the positive aspects of rhetoric and the positive aspects of dialogue. Next, list negative aspects of each. Conduct a conversation to choose which forms of conversation will give the best of each while minimizing the negatives of each. See polarity mapping in Chapter 7.

☐ Based on the input from the group, create a working agreement about when argument is needed and when the group would be more appropriately served by dialogue.

The Overly Articulate

This person is highly articulate, often speaking in elaborate and lengthy paragraphs. Members often experience confusion when this person speaks. While good ideas may be embedded in this person's presentation, they are hard to track and isolate. Frequently the result is either over attention to ferret out meaning or ignoring the contribution and moving on. Here are a few specific interventions to try with this participant type.

- Concisely paraphrase the clearest part of the message or summarize one or two ideas. "Whew, you have a lot to say. Let me see if I can summarize your main point." A clarifying paraphrase requires that they shift from talking to listening. Usually, they will respond with an affirmative or a short clarification of the paraphrase. The important shift is the move from paragraph speech to concise statements of key points.
- Use facilitation moves to balance voices in the room as noted throughout this book. A few techniques include one-minute advocacy (Chapter 7), paraphrase partners (Chapter 7), subject changer (Chapter 6), the monopolizer (Chapter 6), and the know-it-all (Chapter 6).

The Pedagogical Isolate

Occasionally groups encounter a person, often a highly accomplished teacher, who seems to hold disdain for those less knowledgeable or skillful. This person might even articulate that she sees group work as irrelevant and that she has no interest in helping other teachers or the group know what has taken this person so long to develop. Retaining knowledge may, to this person, protect her sense of superiority to the others. Setting the attitude dimension aside, it is true that some people perform better alone than in groups (Nesbitt, 2003). However, collaborative tasks make efforts to include this person's information necessary. Here are some possible approaches.

- When this person speaks, paraphrase with an inquiry for evidence. "Your key point is_____. What is it in your students' learning that is making such a difference?"

- Paraphrase and inquire for a specific point of evidence, which will often cause a shift in thinking and less verbosity. "So you are telling us that the Wonder of Words is the best program you have ever seen. Help us understand a critical element that is different from the program we are using now." To respond, they must stop and think, What is it that is really important?

- Often groups err by trying to do everything as a committee of the whole. Seize opportunities to subgroup members to work on separate tasks and bring the results back to the group.

- Find small parts of the whole that might be useful information and ask the person to contribute. Try priming the person in advance with your request. "I know your PLC is scheduled to talk about _____ today. I'm hoping that more students could benefit from your experience. Would you be willing to share some ideas today?"

- Should you be an administrator in charge of the group, have a conversation with this person, acknowledging her preference to work alone, but insisting that she be a contributing member of the group.

Misinformants

It is important not to let misinformation or extreme minority viewpoints stand as they are because silence implies that all agree with what has been said. Silence does not mean that we agree with the speaker; however, it is sometimes misinterpreted as agreement.

Contested viewpoints need to be made explicit so that agreement is not assumed. The facilitator might try the following:

- Paraphrase the statement and ask, "What other information does the group have on this topic?"
- Reframe the misinformation as a question that moves to the abstract level. For example, "Thelma has stated that we should not let students choose their own books. She is asking a question of censorship. What other questions should we be asking about censorship?"
- Ask the group, "Does anyone have another viewpoint?"
- Poll the group to get a sense of members' views. Say, "Let's see where the group stands. I am going to invite you to go to one of four corners." While pointing at the corners, suggest, "Those who strongly agree with the viewpoint, go here. Those who agree, but not strongly, stand here. Those who disagree, stand here. And those who vehemently disagree with the viewpoint stand here. Go ahead and move to your corners, and then give me your attention." When the group has settled into places, suggest, "Quickly, in your group, summarize what the data tell us, and when I give the signal, sit down." At this point the facilitator has several options:

  - ☐ Do the data warrant more discussion? If so, collect more viewpoints.
  - ☐ If the topic is overworked, requiring the group to move on, comment, "It is clear that we are not going to agree on this topic today. Let's move on."
  - ☐ If the topic is highly contentious, ask for those who have been listening to summarize the different opinions. This helps to neutralize the voice tone and helps

the group hear the issues by saying something like this, "We have three very different opinions. I am going to ask those of you who have been listening to summarize the viewpoints. Who can summarize _____?" Then ask, "Do we need to do something with this information or should we just agree to disagree?"

Interrupters

Sometimes in meetings, one participant will constantly interrupt and become a dominant voice. The facilitator may try the following:

- Insert a structure that sequences turn taking. "Okay, let's hear first from Sarah, then Anthony, and then Maria."
- Recalibrate the working agreement. "You agreed to have one voice in the room at a time. We need to keep that agreement."
- Focus on the issue rather than the offender. "Let's remember to have one person talk at a time and to let people finish their statements."
- Interrupt the interrupter. "Jim, you have a lot of good points, but it is important to let Renee finish, and then I know that Franklin is waiting to say something, as well."

Subject Changers

Group members who continually take the group off topic are similar to interrupters. When they change the subject, the effect is that other group members are distracted. The facilitator works with a subject changer by asking for a relevance check.

- Ask, "Can you help the group understand how your comment relates to the topic?"

- Comment and ask, "This might be taking us away from our topic. What does the group think? Let's hear from a few of you about where we should go next."

- Acknowledge the comment and then note the time, saying, "It is (time), and to accomplish our goal today, we really need to move on."

- Acknowledge the comment and agree to return to the topic later: "I know this is important. Perhaps we can come back to this topic later."

- Acknowledge the comment, set it aside, and move on by saying, "That's an important dimension. Let's add it to the chart here so we can remember to come back to it later. We need to focus on _____ right now." Redirect the group to a tangible third position (such as the agenda) or to a specific topic or speaker who was on topic. Note: Only commit to that which you plan to follow through on. If you do not believe it is worthy of this level of attention, stay with a nonwritten commitment. If it becomes important, it will be brought up again.

Cell Phones and Texting

As of September 2012, 68% of the population earning $75,000 or more had smartphones (Pew Internet, 2012). With the adult population now carrying smartphones, it becomes important to set a working agreement early in the meeting. If the group has time to establish their own agreements, let them set the parameters. If not, set one yourself at the beginning of the meeting. It is helpful to link it to efficiency, such as, "We have a lot to accomplish today, if you have a cell phone in front of you that will distract you, please put it away, and of course, silence the ringer." If someone challenges you, such as, "I need to keep it on because my kids are home alone," ask the group if it would be okay that so-and-so be allowed to keep his phone on silent mode to receive messages. If, as usually happens, someone forgets to comply, simply restate the agreement, "That phone ringing reminds me to have everyone check to make sure their phones are silenced."

If the expectation has been made clear, the ringing of a cell phone alone will embarrass a participant and she will move immediately to silence it. We occasionally might say in response to a ringing phone, "Is that for me?" evoking a laugh and serving as a gentle reminder of the group's agreements about cell phones.

Complete Message—Refinements to the Direct Request

When being directive with a larger group, we advise an expanded version of a *complete message* (see Chapter 4) that includes your personal "I" statement.

- ■ State observable data. "At the last two staff meetings, several people were texting. At least twice, someone had to silence a phone."
- ■ State what you think is the impact on the group. "I think cell phones are disruptive to our group focus, and when some are off task, that slows us down."

or

- ■ State what you think or feel. "When some people follow the rules and put their phones away and others have not, it feels as though we are being rude to ignore agreements we made together."

■ State a need or direction in two steps: Restate the agreement. "We committed to the agreement of being fully present, which means no cell phones or texting at the meeting." Then state the direction. "I need those of you with your cell phones on to comply. Please silence your phone, and put it where it will not distract you."

The first rule of thumb for this message is to craft an effect statement, such as the previous example that focuses on group needs. Sometimes, stating your personal response is the most complete and honest way to address the problem. A participant may need to know that his behavior is irritating, and stating your personal response is the most complete and honest way to address the problem, especially when talking to the person privately. This is particularly important if we find that we cannot, for whatever reason, set aside our emotional response.

SUMMARY

The group behaviors described earlier are often done without conscious awareness of their impact on the group. More often than not, they become habitual and show up consistently in every meeting. By intervening, the facilitator breaks the habit and makes the meeting more efficient by gaining maximum engagement and getting all voices heard, with no one person allowed to dominate. The facilitator not only assists the group in accomplishing its work, but hopefully adds some consciousness to the person whose behavior has been disruptive. People generally do not set out to be disagreeable, but rather do the things they do to take care of some need in the moment. When facilitators remember this, they can intervene neutrally, without judgment and with the respect people deserve.

In the next chapter, we take on the most difficult challenges beginning with some general guidelines, such as bringing the unmentionable to the forefront and then provide some intervention strategies for dealing with particularly difficult participants. One of the most challenging facilitation instances occurs when the facilitator is attacked; not only does the facilitator need to monitor their internal state but also have ways to deflect the attack so that it can be dealt with in a neutral way. The common wisdom of staying calm can work, but sometimes matching energy levels can be more effective.

7

STRATEGIES FOR ADVANCED FACILITATION

_____

S ome group issues seem intractable, and best-laid plans and preemptive actions can derail. Groups with hidden agendas, saboteurs, schoolwide crises, or angry factions are particularly challenging. Sometimes the groups become more and more dysfunctional exhibiting counterproductive behavior, and it is difficult to identify members' positive intentions. In this chapter, we review ways to deal with demoralizing events, disputes, personal attacks, perceived manipulation, and sabotage.

Scott Peck (2003) says that to get to "true community," a place where work is productive and participants are open and honest, the group must work through conflicts. He notes that in his work with groups, participants often avoid conflict by retreating into themselves. Many theorists and practitioners have observed this practice. Peck calls it "pseudocommunity." Others describe this tendency as the "Thumper Theory" inspired by the movie *Bambi:* "If you can't say something nice, don't say something at all." Michael Fullan (1991) describes this avoidance behavior in elementary schools as returning to the "individual egg crate" or in high schools, the "creation of Balkan States" or silos of the like-minded. Bob Chadwick (2010), an old growth forest ranger turned skilled conflict resolver, reminds us that we all have a personal relationship with conflict—some of us avoid it at all costs, others relish the drama, and a few may want to heighten the conflict. Few know how to turn it into productive energy; these abilities clearly separate the novice from the accomplished facilitator.

The challenge for facilitators and group members is to learn to manage conflict and to use it productively to find new solutions. Accomplished facilitators do not shy away from conflict and know that when skillfully handled, it adds value to the community. (For more information see the free resource *Beyond Conflict to Consensus: An Introductory Learning Manual* by Bob Chadwick, 2010.)

The skilled facilitator has learned how to harness the energy of conflict to help others learn more about themselves and one another. We will address nine issues that are challenges even for experienced facilitators:

1. Group conflict

2. Demoralizing external events

3. Disputes

4. Dissenting views

5. Personal attacks

6. Challenges to the leader

7. Subgroup manipulation

8. Sabotage

9. Irresolvable conflict

GROUP CONFLICT

Sometimes complex problems can emotionally and cognitively overwhelm a group. In these circumstances, give rich rationale for the specific and detailed process steps you present. The what-why-how pattern described in Chapter 4 is essential here. Use scaffolds to simplify tasks such as writing out steps, checking for understanding, clearly identifying roles, and so forth.

Conflict specialist Jennifer Abrams reported this situation to us. Teachers were disagreeing about the district's directive to follow the new grading policy, accept the new course descriptions (and teach to them), and create common assessments. Resistance abounded. Some people viewed alignment as an affront to their personal expertise; others resisted working together so they wouldn't agree to meet to work on the courses; and yet others wanted to see more research before they would agree to any of the expectations. Emotions ran high. Teachers had not been involved in the original decision making; some were satisfied with the status quo, others felt the workload was increasing beyond reasonable expectations.

Abrams (2009) stresses the importance of clear outcomes as a critical element before moving to specific plans. When outcomes are clear, plans and processes can be more flexible. Early outcomes must include helping people get to manageable emotional states. Provide clear and specific process tools. Open the meeting with a grounding, the best equalizer we know to prepare for difficult conversations. This strategy sets norms for everyone being heard, allows the expression of feelings and thinking, and establishes a safe environment for conflict. We repeat the instructions here from Chapter 4 for reader convenience.

Grounding

- If the group is large, break members into groups of six to eight with a mechanism for reporting out at the end of the small group interactions.
- Explain that the purpose of the activity is to establish a norm for respectful listening.
- Explain the procedure, and post on a flip chart what members will talk about.

  - ☐ My name is . . .
  - ☐ My relationship to this topic is . . .
  - ☐ My expectations are . . .
  - ☐ How I feel about being here is . . .

- When members indicate that they understand the process, name the first speaker in each group, and have group members then take turns speaking.
- Ask that when one member speaks, all others remain silent.
- Ask group members to give full nonverbal attention to the speaker.
- After everyone in the small group has spoken, have the first speaker summarize to the group what has been said.
- When all groups are finished, call on the first speaker in each group to give a summary statement to the full assembly.

Since the primary purpose of grounding is to give participants an opportunity to be heard, be sure members do not feel rushed. In the previous example, to save time, the large group was broken into subgroups. However, the more challenging the topic, the more valuable a full-group grounding. With a group size of 40 to 50 people, this activity might take as long as an hour. Another useful multistep process is to create a desired state map. In some cases, the facilitator may plan to use both interventions.

Existing State–Desired State

When groups focus on the desired state, their work is most expedient and productive. If a group already knows about the issues, spending time on the existing state can be counterproductive and drag groups down emotionally. Instead of dissecting the problem and causing the group to perseverate on negativity, we advise giving limited attention to the existing state.

Two exceptions to this principle are when group members do not have enough information about the problem or when the emotions are high. For example, we once worked to resolve issues associated with substitute teachers. It turns out that each constituent—teachers, substitutes, administration—interacted around the issues in a different way, and each group had their own set of assumptions about the problem. In this case, each group needed more information about the others' viewpoints, and they all needed to identify their existing problem. In addition, if emotions are strong and a facilitator moves too quickly to solution, the group will be resistant to the invitation to move to desired state. When emotions are high, it is important to pace this existing emotional state. (We describe this in more detail later in the chapter.) Once the desired state has been defined, the intervention needs to focus on the internal resources needed—knowledge, skills, and attitude. Figure 7.1 shows a desired state map that the reader will find useful as you consider these examples.

Figure 7.1 Desired State Map

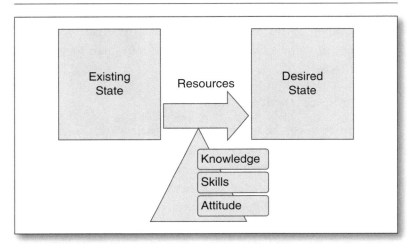

The desired state map can be used in at least two ways: as a personal planning tool for a group or as a consulting/coaching tool.

1. Personal planning tool for a group. In planning for an upcoming meeting, a facilitator might reflect on the last meeting and realize that most of the conversation was dominated by three people (existing state) and that the desired state was to have a balance of voices in the conversations. Her desired state become an interactive meeting with all voices participating. She might direct her planning to her own internal resources.

   ■ *Knowledge.* An intervention was needed and the situation needed to be handled in a way that provided dignity for all participants.
   ■ *Skill.* Use pair-share more often, and ask for comments from people who have not yet spoken. Ask the group

to paraphrase the various positions. Employ satisfy, satisfy, delay, and engage mental rehearsal about these strategies.

■ *Attitude.* Personal confidence and positive presuppositions about the vocal members.

2. As a consulting/coaching tool. Bob was once contracted to consult with and coach an assistant superintendent (AS) who without realizing it was interacting with school and community leaders and creating political harm for the superintendent (existing state). While the AS was an extremely competent, organized, detail-oriented person, she seemed to have limited human relationship skills. In a joint intake meeting, the superintendent explained that he wanted to support the AS in correcting her performance and that improvement was a condition of her continued employment. He asked if she was willing to work with Bob for support. Bob met with her for three one-hour meetings.

At the first meeting, they looked at a display of the desired state map. Bob reviewed the complaints the superintendent was receiving, stated that the desired state was that the AS's actions support the superintendent and foster positive relationships with the community. With the assistant leading, the two brainstormed indicators of the desired state. Here is some of what they listed:

Clients would request services from the AS, invite her to meetings, thank her for contributions, and ask her opinion in meetings. They would feel valued, feel welcomed, feel respected, feel comfortable, and feel efficacious in relationship with both the superintendent and the community.

As the AS worked to develop this list, she was developing insights about her behavior and discovered that her behavior needed to provide clients the opportunities to experience all the attributes of the desired state. Given this realization, they begin to list the resources needed for the AS to accomplish this desired state.

Knowledge. Aware of what behaviors were causing the problem and what behaviors could replace the problematic ones.

Skills. Paraphrase, inquire, balance credible and approachable voice, and skills at building relationships with individuals and small groups.

Attitude. Competence didn't mean control and relationships are important to getting work done.

The last meeting focused on what specific behaviors she could do to have clients feel valued, feel welcomed, feel respected, feel comfortable, feel efficacious in relationship with both the superintendent and the community. She kept her job.

DEMORALIZING EXTERNAL EVENTS

Schools regularly adopt new programs, change assessments, reorganize schedules, revise curriculum, reinvigorate instruction, or change personnel. In any change, simple or more complex, staff must traverse psychological transition zones (Bridges, 1980). Some events are so shocking and outside of the group's control that the event disrupts equilibrium, reduces efficacy, and wreaks emotional havoc. A school closing, student's or faculty member's sudden death, a fire, an angry public, a work slowdown or strike—all these constitute some level of crisis that shocks the mind and creates excessive stress.

The facilitator's job in these situations is to respectfully reflect group members' emotions and concerns and also redirect the energy to a productive path and lead them to resourceful states of mind. In this section, we review four tools: redirecting mental energy to a neutral third point, using a fourth point to manage resistance, a pace-and-lead procedure to reframe mental states, and structured interviews.

Third Point

Using a third point allows the facilitator to be tough on ideas but soft on people. This move also serves to deflect an attack by moving "the problem" to an inanimate third point, such as another space in the room. As an example, a group member, Jake, had made a pointed attack on another group member whom he felt did not hold up his share of the bargain. A facilitator might say, "Jake, let me state the problem as I see it. You are describing an issue that deals with how we make commitments. Let's take it out of the personal (gesture with palm down toward the group), and deal with it as *a problem we want to solve* (create a third point by gesturing with palm up toward a neutral space, such as an easel). To the entire group the facilitator asks, "How do you want to address issues about keeping commitments?"

On one occasion when Diane was a principal, she found herself under attack in a public meeting from a parent group who were blaming her for a poor choice made by a teacher. Diane knew she needed to get out of the hot seat and used a third point to move the attack to a neutral space. She stated, "I feel that I am under attack, and for me to be able to listen to you, I need to put the problem here." (She picked up the empty chair next to her and set it down in a new space.) While touching the chair (the new third point) she continued, "Tonight you have come to me with concerns about our social studies curriculum that you believe is racist. Let's identify the issues. I need to be able to clearly articulate your issues to my staff. I know your concerns are serious."

First-, Second-, Third-, and Fourth-Point Communication

When conflicts are high, the skilled facilitator wants to carefully identify who or what is involved; Zoller (2010, p. 30) describes a useful way of framing communication using four points and pairing these points to congruent gestures. One-point communication strengthens an "I" message by referring and gesturing toward one's self. Two-point communication is inclusive in that it includes another person or a group. When referring to this relationship, move the arm from the self to the other or the group to communicate this inclusion. The third-point communication, as noted previously, directs attention away from the people in the room, usually to a neutral object or space in the room, such as an easel, a chair, or a document. Finally, Zoller identifies a fourth point, which directs the attention to a person, place, event, or thing not present in the room. This can be helpful when needing to deflect some of the emotion to outside the room. It also can be used to make the point that we can only work with what we have in the room at the time, not phantom fourth parties. Zoller also points out that the fourth point can be used to name resistance.

Zoller (2010) notes that when gesturing, a loosely cupped hand is more inviting than a pointed finger. When the palm is held up, it invites; when it is held down, it signals that you want to negate or stop something. Note in the previous example about Jake, the facilitator gestures with a palm down to signal the need to move on from the personal attack to solving the problem in which the palm is then turned up as an invitation.

Redirect Resistance

When an external event disrupts equilibrium, some group members may resist change and the group cannot move forward. The facilitator can help to redirect that resistance with respectful language that addresses the root of the issue. For example, a facilitator might say, "Some of you may be thinking, 'What are we doing in a meeting when we could be in classrooms getting ready for the school year?'" The facilitator stands in a space away from the group and points beyond the wall at the classrooms (a fourth point). Next, the facilitator moves in toward the group and gestures with open hands, saying, "At the same time, some of you probably are curious about what can be so important that we need to meet now and what might you be able to do to resolve the problem."

Zoller (2010) teaches that in addition to gesture, the nuances of language matter when forming a statement describing feelings in the group. "I can imagine that some of you are feeling uncomfortable with this news." Acknowledging emotional states validates personal experiences and neutralizes possible resistance. The facilitator's comment needs to be designed to most accurately reflect group members' various experiences and often includes a statement of possible emotions. Consider these gradations of inclusiveness and certainty:

- All of you (will, might)
- Some of you might
- All of us
- Some of us
- A part of you
- A part of us

Putting It All Together

To keep a group resourceful and to redirect resistance, we describe how a colleague effectively applied all of the skills described so far in this chapter. Her outcome was to deliver bad news about audit findings to a group, and then engage their support in working productively on solutions. As she moved to this item on the agenda, she purposefully situated herself away from center front and while holding up the audit report she emphasized, "These are the results of the external audit (tangible third point). This audit tells us what experts outside of this room have observed." She now gestures toward a space outside of the room creating that invisible fourth point. "These experts are critical of our school and find faults with some of our methods." She then pauses, holds the document down at her side, and comments on possible reactions. "Many of you will have emotional responses to this report. Some of you may feel angry, frustrated, or unappreciated" (pacing statement). She then moves to the center of the room and sets the report down on a table far to the right of her. Gesturing both palms out and up toward the group (inviting second position), "Our job is to figure out how to respond to the conclusions drawn in the report while maintaining our integrity as the professionals that we know we are. There is much to digest, and we will only get started today." Finally, she concludes by holding her palm facing her chest (first point), and states, "My job is to help us understand the information provided and find productive ways so that we can continue on our journey to be the best that we can."

Not only did this administrator use gesture to mark the different levels of responsibility, she effectively separated the different messages by using space to communicate the changes. By keeping the bad news off to the side and then moving back to center when she wanted to move to productive messages, she facilitated the psychological shift that is necessary when working with resistance, or for that matter, any strong emotion. She helped the group separate the bad news as something they needed to address; helped the group understand that she was the carrier of the message, not the message; and that it was her job to help them deal with the disturbing message in a productive way.

Pace and Lead

In *Cognitive Coaching,* Costa and Garmston (2002) teach a strategy called *pace and lead.* Pacing means matching the group's experience or emotional tone using direct statements, paraphrasing, or story. The pace acknowledges the validity of group members' emotional states, contributes to rapport, and makes possible movement to another emotional space. The pattern consists of sensory verifiable statements (pace) followed by a positive suggestion (lead). This pattern is the basis for virtually all successful communication, which seeks to influence.

Notice that in the Putting It All Together example, the administrator paced the group when she said, "Some of you may feel angry, frustrated, or unappreciated," and then she offered a lead by inviting them to consider ways that they can work productively together.

To provide another example, Bob describes how he met with an elementary school staff to review the results of sensing interviews. The sensing interview protocol had him ask each member three questions: (1) What are you feeling good about in this school? (2) What concerns do you have? (3) What recommendations do you have?

Alerted that this staff had a reputation of blaming the principal for everything and taking no responsibility themselves, Bob started the session with a story that paced the existing condition and lead to a desired emotional stage for the group. "Hi. Before we start, I am wondering if anyone has heard about the children's story *How Green Is My Garden?* In the story, a man lives on a little planet and asks an expert to come in and assess how well his garden is growing. The expert is puzzled because he seems to be getting the same information from different plants, but in very different ways. Some plants accuse the gardener of being inattentive, leaving the water on so long it floods their roots and being insensitive to the location of their roots when he hoes, sometimes nicking them. (Bob reports their data in a whiney voice.) Other plants give the same information but in a different way. They say the gardener is not careful about the watering, and the plants have to yell at him telling him enough already and please shut off the water now. (Bob raises his voice slightly.) The expert considers what he is hearing and is puzzled about what is going on. Finally, he realizes what it is. Both sets of plants have the same data but some are reporting it in ways that permit something to be done about it."

In this story, Bob (paced) described the existing behavior of the group (complaining and blaming) and (lead) described desired behavior (taking responsibility for communicating responsibly). At some level, the group knew he was talking about them. They rose to the occasion and demonstrated responsible behavior during the meeting as they examined data from the sensing interviews.

Structured Interviews

Often, change comes to school programs like an avalanche disturbing the geography in which teachers work. Groups need help managing both their emotional responses to the changes in addition to developing programmatic adjustments. Bob and Carolyn McKanders, a director of Thinking Collaborative, once worked with an urban school that was experiencing a change in leadership, a turnover in one-third of the staff, a dramatic increase in the number of students, and added classrooms. In *Anticipate Change: Design a Transition Meeting* (Garmston, 2004), Bob describes three outcomes in their work:

(1) Enhance the staff's capacity to cope with change.

(2) Help staff members see change as an opportunity for school improvement.

(3) Increase staff members' sense of power and control over elements of the change.

In the structured interview approach, groups of six are formed and numbered off, each with one question about which they will interview other members of the group. Each has a recording sheet. Six rounds are held as follows:

- In the first round, members interview themselves writing their response to the question they are investigating. In the second round, Members 1 and 2 interview each other, Members 3 and 4 interview each other, and Members 5 and 6 interview each other. In the third round, regroup: Members 1 and 3 interview each other, Members 2 and 5 interview each other, and Members 4 and 6 interview each other. In the fourth round, regroup: Members 1 and 4 interview each other, Members 2 and 6 interview each other, and Members 3 and 5 interview each other. In round five, the pairs are Members 1 and 5, Members 2 and 4, and Members 3 and 6. In the final round, Members 1 and 6, Members 2 and 3, and Members 4 and 5 are paired.

- After the sixth round, members join others with the same interview question, share, chart their results, and prepare to report to the full group. The questions used for this interview were the following:

  □ What is over, and what is not?
  □ What do you value and want to continue?
  □ As individuals and as a group, what can we do to support ourselves through changes?
  □ What are some areas in which we might need to tap into our creativity?
  □ What are some areas in which we might need to manage the chaos of transition?
  □ If this phase of our school's life looks like clouds, what might be some silver linings?

DISPUTES

Conflict in meetings can be productive, especially cognitive conflict—disagreement about ideas (Amason, Thompson, Hochwarter, & Harrison, 1995). New ideas can emerge when the energy of such conflict is funneled into developing constructive solutions. However, some of the disputes that occur in meetings can become personal. They may be caused by private agendas, stylistic differences, power, fear, and competition for scarce resources. Throughout disputes, the effective facilitator is careful to remain neutral. To help the group, the facilitator may try the following:

Stop the Dispute Early

As soon as the discussion becomes unconstructive or insulting, jump in and intervene with either of these options:

- ■ "I don't think we are going to resolve your disagreement at this point, so I am going to ask that we move on. Daphne and Leo may want to talk about this in private."
- ■ "A norm for working through conflict is to discuss issues, not people. Your passion shows; however, we need to stick with the issue. Let's take a moment and ask the group to summarize the issues on the table. Can someone help paraphrase for us?"

Verbalize the Issue

Try to understand the emotional impact that the situation is creating and express this viewpoint.

- ■ "Some may feel anxious and uncertain about what we are doing here. Let's list the pros and cons for each position."

Acknowledge Each Position

The facilitator can help neutralize the situation by recognizing aloud participants' differing points of view:

- "We have reached a tough sticking point. It seems some of you think we need to invite parents, and others think we should not."

- "Some of you want everyone to be involved and think that is important for group cohesion; others of you think it should be left to individual choice, as the demands are already too time consuming. What middle ground might we find?" (This strategy has the logical structure of *not A or B but C*.)

- Summarize the conflict and ask, "Our conflict seems to be about how to best assess our progress. I need other ideas from the whole group as to how to proceed."

- Acknowledge the disagreement and agree to move on. Try saying, "We have some agreement about how to measure our progress. In the time we have left, I believe we need to spell out what we will do between now and our next meeting."

Identify the Sources of Information

Ask each person the source of his or ideas. For example, say, "Help us understand what led you to this conclusion."

Check Perceptions

Refer to a posted statement. "Today there seems to be an agreement about how to sequence the work. Jackie, is that your perception of the agreement?"

Reframe the Conflict as an Asset

Tell the group that conflict is a healthy part of group dynamics and can enhance individuals' learning and the quality of decisions they make. Present the research finding that productive groups have conflict about ideas, but minimize interpersonal conflict (Amason et al., 1995).

- Have group members turn to a partner and see if each pair can summarize what they believe are the key points of the conflict. Give the group enough time to summarize, but not so much time that they begin to debate the issues.
- Structure the way group members report out by giving both sides an opportunity to talk without repeating what has already been said. A facilitator might say, "In this next process, each group will put their ideas on the table. Listen carefully so that if your group has additional information you can add it. There will be no need to repeat what has already been said." Closure is not always necessary during this meeting. It may be useful to let the various ideas percolate until a later meeting.

DISSENTING VIEWS

When dissenting views become too dominant, other participants stop listening or trying to understand. In this case, the facilitator must be even more vigilant about skillfully paraphrasing what is said, giving dissenting opinions or ideas equal weight to legitimize them as options to be considered. The facilitator's carefully mediated approach models a way to agree to disagree without destroying the conversation.

Disagreements can morph into contention—a desire to win at any cost. Advise members that four natural tendencies can render them less effective and successful in resolving their differences: (1) a natural desire to explain my side first, (2) ineffective listening, (3) fear that we will not get our way, and (4) the assumption that one of us has to lose. Given these inclinations, encourage people to paraphrase one another, and learn to trust that these processes will help bring satisfaction to multiple points of view.

Facilitators will want to consistently model paraphrasing as a useful tool when dissenting views are present. For example, a facilitator might paraphrase and then say, "I hear two main ideas in the room. Let's bring it back to center. Where do we need to go next?" Several strategies can serve to redirect the conversation when dissent is keeping the group from working well. Try these approaches.

Paraphrase Partner

When two people engage in destructive verbal volleying, establish a paraphrase partner for each speaker. Ask, "Can someone summarize the key points of view for _____? Thanks, Andre, now I need someone to summarize the key points for ____. Thanks, Charlotte." After a few exchanges, while they may still not agree, each party typically will begin to hear the other's intention without the negative connotations.

Pace the Emotion

Respect the emotion of the attacking person. Assume that a speaker in attack mode may be protecting himself. Say something like, "This is really upsetting to you, and it is important that we understand. Group, please turn to a partner and clarify for yourself the two conflicting points of view."

Redirect the Attacks

■ Use a third-point communication. Point to a chart on which the conflicting views are recorded and ask, "Given those views, what are the sticking points?"

■ Use a fourth-point communication: Move to a wall and point beyond the room. Say, "That is an issue that is being worked on in the legislature." Move back into the room to the facilitator's place before continuing, "Our task today is _____."

Reframe the Opposition

Recast the issue as one of personal style, a subset of behavior, rather than the whole person.

■ "Each of you has a style that drives the way that you think about issues. Notice that Thomas often looks at the opposite side of things. This is a thinking style, and it can be helpful to have a voice that examines ideas with a critical eye. I propose that each time before you speak over the next 10 minutes, you consider your style and how your style shapes what you are about to say. Then challenge yourself to reframe the comment using a different style."

Helping Groups Use Styles

■ DeBono's (1985) six thinking hats are a useful and productive diagnostic tool that help participants understand the various roles of participants. In dysfunctional groups, a few participants

(Continued)

(Continued)

take on some of these roles and play them repeatedly like broken records. It is freeing to know that others will sometimes wear the red hat and respond emotionally as well. The hats are as follows:

(1) Adding information (white hat)

(2) Responding with feelings, hunches, or intuition (red hat)

(3) Judging comments (black hat)

(4) Talking about the bright side (yellow hat)

(5) Suggesting alternatives or new ideas (green hat)

(6) Pushing the thinking processes (blue hat)

Using the hats as intervention strategies:

- ■ "When I paraphrase, I am going to mention your thinking hat: Julie is wearing the red hat when she tells us so passionately how excited she is about _____."
- ■ "Before you speak, tell us which hat you are wearing and then give us your idea. This will help us to know more about your thinking on the topic."

When the facilitator makes group members conscious of their personal styles, they learn more about themselves and begin to appreciate how various styles can contribute to, rather than distract from, group work. Sometimes dissenting views are so entangled that they deserve a block of time, or even the entire meeting, before the group will be ready to move on. With this in mind, the facilitator needs to provide time in the agenda to help the group work through emotions and ideas, especially when the group is being polarized. The following activities are designed to help groups unpack their thinking:

Create an Assumptions Wall

Divide the group into smaller groups of 6 to 12 people, and have the groups unpack the underlying suppositions or assumptions behind each position using an assumptions wall. Participants often will find points in common or recognize misunderstandings that can be cleared up. To create an assumptions wall, do the following:

■ Individuals list assumptions about a topic.
■ Individuals then choose one that most informs their behavior.
■ Group members write their choice on a sentence strip in 8 to 12 words.
■ All groups post their assumptions on the wall.
■ The facilitator models inquiry, saying, for example, "I'm curious about that assumption. Whose is it? Help me to understand some reasons you value that highly."
■ Individuals inquire about posted assumptions in a round-robin fashion.
■ Caution the group not to spend too much time on the first assumption being explored.
■ Intervene and refocus the group when the inquiry begins to sound like an interrogation.

Brainstorm Questions

Identify the issue. Ask small groups to brainstorm questions and to write them on sentence strips to be posted. Then have participants put up their question and read it to the group. Check to see if other groups asked a variation on this question. Compare the questions and choose the one that seems most essential to work on. Move on to the next question or list the top three questions as the group's agenda.

Metaphor

Once when Diane was working with a group, they got into a huge conflict whether books students were reading needed to be previewed in advance. The dispute became heated quickly with two staff members ready to face off with each other. Diane used the following intervention steps that should be familiar to the reader by now:

■ To pace the experience, she borrowed a story from Native American lore about how the coyote is a trickster that enters the room and plays havoc with groups. She noted, "The coyote has just come into our room and created conflict. He is tricking us into thinking that we should have answers, but really his message is that we need to ask better questions. The gift of the coyote is knowing that he plays paradoxical roles—he is both a trickster and a messenger. He is telling us to slow down and frame our issues before we go on."

■ To neutralize the conflict and create a third point, Diane wrote "censorship" on the chart. She then stated, "I am going to suggest that our real issue is about censorship. One viewpoint thinks we need to censor everything, limiting choice to what is in the library. The other thinks that students can be responsible for choosing books and that they can use the teachable moment to handle any issues that might come up."

■ She then directed the group with a lead, "We will not have time to solve this problem today, but we can start to ask good questions. Turn to those at your table group and decide what questions we need to be asking about censorship. We only have about five minutes to spend on this today." She placed special emphasis on censorship to emphasize the neutral third point.

▨ After five minutes, she gave a signal, and then asked the participants to share their questions, which she captured on chart paper.

▨ She then transitioned back to the meeting. As she rolled up the charts, she commented, "We will take a look at these in leadership team and decide what our next steps need to be in the future."

Disperse to Agree

When the group has talked at length about seemingly intractable problems, have a representative of each viewpoint step out of the room with instructions to come back to the group when the representatives have reached a solution. Have the larger group commit ahead of time to whatever solution the representatives devise.

PERSONAL ATTACKS

Sometimes dissenting views become personal attacks, and any of the strategies in this chapter can be appropriate. Sometimes, however, riskier acts are necessary to protect individuals in the group.

The Six-Step Response

Chapter 1 opens with the story of an algebra teacher who shouted out during a session, "This has nothing to do with algebra." This is a high-risk situation for the facilitator and group—safety has been challenged. The chapter details six steps the facilitator can take to defuse the situation.

1. Move

2. Ask the person's name

3. Paraphrase in the person's own intonation

4. Make a polite inquiry as to the nature of the person's problem. If not resolved at this step, move on.

5. Ask if the person is willing to wait for a break time conversation with the facilitator.

6. If not, suggest the person has a choice—to stay in the room and try to get value out of what is happening or leave the room to do something of greater value to his algebra students than being here. Assure the person you will support him whatever he chooses.

Step Between Opposing Members

▨ If possible, break eye contact by stepping between the speaker and the person being verbally attacked. Turn your body two-thirds toward the victim while keeping a peripheral eye on the attacker. Say, "This has pushed a button. Can someone in the group paraphrase the issue in a way that is less emotional?"

▨ Or step between them and paraphrase the speaker's comment to show its positive intention without the negativity. "I think Cecelie is trying to tell us that she does not agree with the direction we are taking. Let's slow down and see if we can find out more about why she and others might disagree. Can anyone shed light on this issue?" By asking the group to respond, it defuses the conflict between the two parties. If no one responds, redirect the group to paraphrase what they perceive the conflict to be. Then inquire to seek more understanding about the issues the group raises.

Change the Narrative

- Offer a "saving face narrative" when a member breaks down in the meeting. For example, you might say, "Rosa has had a whole life of prejudice. Something that is happening here may be triggering that for her. Breakdowns are going to happen from time to time, and we need to respect that and provide the space where she can regain her dignity. Let's give her some private time while we move on."

Enlist the Group in Solving the Problem

- Ask the group to problem solve: "I notice that the group seems upset by the negative interchanges that are occurring. Turn to a partner and see if one of our working agreements would help us reframe the issues." If none of them are obvious ask, "What new working agreement might we need?"

CHALLENGES TO THE LEADER

To be effective, the facilitator must maintain rapport, trust, and control over processes. When any of these are threatened, the group feels unsafe, and the leader runs the risk of losing emotional centeredness. As noted in Chapter 2, the facilitator needs to first monitor her internal state by breathing, being grounded, and stepping to a new spot before deciding what to do next.

Use a Process Commercial

Sometimes groups argue about suggested processes. Arguments about process are no-win situations and can absorb much of the group's time. The facilitator's goal is to move the group out of the mire and into productive work.

- "It doesn't matter which road we take; either will get us there. Are you willing to give this a try?"
- "Can you give us permission to try it, and if it is not working, we can change it?"
- If the group still is reluctant, just go with the group's alternative idea.

Sometimes, one group member may be particularly belligerent, such as in the example in Chapter 1. We have witnessed a meeting in which an angry participant stood up and said, "Why are you leading this meeting?" When a group member challenges the facilitator directly about his leadership, the facilitator needs to find an appropriate way to engage with the speaker without becoming flustered and also saving face for all involved.

Engage With More Intensity

- Here is a multistep process that raises the intensity and then steps it down in the redirect. Paraphrase in a way that matches the speaker's vocal intensity: "So you are wondering why I am leading this meeting." Then lead to a new direction using a credible voice, "The question of leadership is important, and it is essential that the group feel the facilitator can be fair and neutral. Thanks for raising the question."

- Continuing with a credible voice explain, "Facilitation can help the group use time more efficiently and complete tasks in a timely way."
- Explain, "My service as a facilitator is of greater value to the group than my participation in the conversation."
- Acknowledge, "Many in the room could facilitate as well as I can. I volunteered because I felt I could stay neutral on the content and thought I could help the group work efficiently on the agenda."
- Ask with an approachable voice, but shift to the second point, "What other reservations might the group have about facilitation?"

Engage With Less Intensity

Here is a list of individual moves to try. The facilitator is always seeking an intervention that models civil conversation, which is what is wanted.

- Paraphrase: "So you disagree with _____." Acknowledge: "Alternative views can be helpful (with a credible voice that drops at the end). Let's keep this in mind as we move on."
- Make a polite inquiry, "What is it about this that is troubling you?"
- Ask, "Is your objection based on a principle or preference?"
- If it is a principle ask, "Can you elaborate?"
- If it is a preference, ask, "In the interest of time, are you willing to move on?" or state, "In the interest of time, we need to move on."

Request Civility

If the comments made to the facilitator are out of bounds and simply rude, the facilitator should set the tone for a civil conversation by using a version of pacing and leading as described previously.

- ▪ Paraphrase, nearly matching the angry tone of the participant, "You're feeling angry!"
- ▪ Focus on listening: "I am having difficulty hearing your message because your voice tone feels like an attack. Can you state your need in a more neutral tone?"
- ▪ "As a participant you every right to feel that way, but no right to express it in an offensive manner. Can you restate your objection more politely?"

It can be helpful to break the pattern of conversation between the facilitator and the rude participant by creating an opportunity for small groups to have a conversation before moving back to whole group interaction.

SUBGROUP MANIPULATION

When a few people outside the meeting try to manipulate decisions and make an end run around democratic processes, the facilitator uses processes to encourage everyone to work together honestly and cooperatively.

Set aside time to review the agenda early in meetings and make sure that all important decisions are made near the beginning when everyone is there.

Suggest a new working agreement of "suspension of judgment," which requires that each person stay open to changing his mind during the course of the discussion based on his own honest assessment of the value of ideas presented and the merit of each solution.

When the facilitator senses that a subgroup may attempt an end-run around the group process or that some members may have met ahead of time to form a position on a decision, the facilitator may wish to structure seating so that conspirators are not seated together. Next, use a decision-making strategy that disaggregates the question.

Decision Matrix to Rank Priorities

Matrices disaggregate problems by helping groups focus on multiple options, moving them away from polarities and toward effective communication. In this example, a superintendent worked with a district leadership team to decide priorities for their yearly staff development calendar. As per contract, the teachers' union and the administrative team had generated the original list. For purposes of example here, we use a partial list.

To create a decision matrix, list options in the first column. In the next two columns, using the rankings of high (H), medium (M), and low (L), list the group ranking for the importance of each option and their assessment of their performance. At each step, invite members to inquire about the reasoning of others to keep the group in dialogue. As in the next example, when the group does not have consensus, give the item a temporary double ranking, and then return at the end of the discussion to check for consensus. In the next case, the group agreed to give ELD a medium ranking because through dialogue they realized that thinking maps were considered a powerful ELD intervention. This one realization brought the group to a quick consensus and demonstrated the power of this type of decision-making tool.

If the group is ready to rank, but there still seems to be some disagreement, ask the group to complete a silent ballot as a litmus test to ascertain how close they are to agreement. Use the sufficient consensus rule, 80%, to prevent one or two dissenting views from holding up decision making.

Figure 7.2 Importance and Performance Decision Matrix

Option	Importance to Us	Our Performance	Ranking
A—Parent Communications	H	M	4
B—English Language Development (ELD)	M (originally double ranked H–M)	M	3
C—New Writing Program	H	L	1
D—Thinking Maps	M	L	2

Values Decision Matrix

A values decision matrix adds criteria based on group values to assess the options. In the abbreviated example in Figure 7.3, we see a representative group of teachers who were vested to recommend a supplemental writing program.

In this example, the group was able to see their priorities and their dialogue led them to a recommendation that the

Figure 7.3 Values Decision Matrix

Options	Values				Ranking
	Supports Standards	Time to Implement	Provides Examples of Good Writing From Literature	Innovative	
Designs for Writing	H	M	H	H	1
Write Tools	M	H	M	M	2
Odyssey Writer	L	H	L	H	3

district consider purchasing their top two choices because both programs filled gaps in the current writing program. They also agreed that because Odyssey Writer did not support the standards well and would take a lot of time to implement because of the technology component, this was not a viable option. The power of this matrix is that it supports values-based decision making.

Require a Quorum

If necessary, create a working agreement that requires that a quorum be present when the group makes decisions, and insist that only decisions recorded in the meeting minutes be accepted as valid.

Pace, Lead, and Poll

Suggest to the group that more discussion may be needed. Try a statement such as, "It appears that some of you are ready to make a decision and others are not (pacing their experience). What you want is a choice you can all live with and that satisfies the group's goals (leading to the desired state). Let's check in with the group and see if we need more discussion. Give a thumbs up if you are ready to move on, a thumb sideways if you need more discussion." Follow the group's will.

One-Minute Advocacy

Clearly defining the space for dialogue and decision making helps groups stay clear about communicative roles. By separating advocacy from inquiry (see Chapter 3), participants not only listen differently, they are more willing to speak up. One-minute advocacy works as follows:

- Identify that the period for advocacy is now open.
- Set the ground rules: (1) only one idea at a time; (2) keep the advocacy short (no more than a minute); (3) if you wish to speak more than once, you need to allow another to speak again before you do; (4) the advocacy will go as long as there are more than two people who wish to speak; (5) if the advocacy slips into a dyadic advocacy between just a few of you, I will intervene and ask the group if we are ready to make a decision.
- At the end of the advocacy, signal the close by holding your hands out as if holding an invisible beach ball. As you bring your hands together say, "The time for advocacy is closing." This gives the facilitator a chance to scan the

group to see if there is anyone who might want to speak up, but seems to be holding back.

- Move to consensus building or a vote as appropriate.

We have found that this use of short advocacies effectively balances voices in the room and builds groups' feelings of efficacy. As one teacher put it, "Our staff used to debate *ad nauseum*. Sometimes, we'd even forget what was important. Now we have lively advocacy. We get things done, and quite frankly, I think we make better decisions."

Alternate Microphones Advocacy

When the group is large, establish two speaking spaces—one for those in favor of a proposition and one for those dissenting. Invite proponents to line up to speak behind these spaces. Set clear ground rules ahead of time: (1) statements should be brief and directed toward issues, not people; (2) limit advocacies to a minute or limit input to one idea at a time; (3) those wishing to speak more than once can get in line again to speak on another topic; (4) no limit to the number of times you are in line, unless you are the only one left. We observed this process at the annual meeting of the California School Employee's Association (CSEA) annual meeting where more than 1,000 delegates effectively dealt with a complex agenda about proposed policy changes. Since then, we have used it on a much smaller scale. The beauty of this structured advocacy is that it balances voices in the room. Often, verbal participants find out that others have the same ideas and are willing to speak up if the structures are safe. In the CSEA meeting, the debate stopped when one line disappeared, also an effective way to stop over-dominance by one group.

SABOTAGE

When group members agree publicly and then criticize privately, the facilitator must decide how severe and persistent the sabotage is to determine whether and how to address it. Responses to this challenge range from light to full calorie.

- Acknowledge that many thoughts often are unspoken in meetings because people fear some statements might offend others or hurt the leader. Try assuring the group that bringing issues forward is needed to help make things better. Remind the group that the sum of the parts is greater than the whole—that getting everyone's ideas and responses in the group can help resolve issues.
- Surface tensions by asking what another stakeholder such as parents or the district office might say about the issue.
- Be generous and consider that cynics often are frustrated optimists and that sabotage is their response to a broken system full of disappointment for someone who was once an optimist. Think of them as allies and spend time both inside and outside of meetings seeking to learn more about their viewpoints, not with the idea of changing them, but to better understand them. Often, these voices of dissent bring forth niggling problems that when considered as part of the solution are additive and create more robust solutions. Just as we described how coyote can be helpful, consider the cynic as the voice of dissent.
- When the group is at the point of making an agreement, ask participants to pair up to explore what it would take

for them to sabotage the agreement. Have the pairs report. Verbalizing potential sabotage surfaces real tensions in the direction the group has selected and can help identify practical responses to some of those tensions.

- Ask group members to explore with a partner what might be talked about in the parking lot after the meeting. Have members report and suggest ways to address concerns.
- Introduce an elephant walk, using the metaphor that there is an elephant in the boardroom and no one mentions it. Ask members to walk around the room and share with one another unspoken issues that might exist. When the group reassembles, ask table groups to share their findings and then to report.

IRRESOLVABLE CONFLICT

Some problems cannot be solved, only managed. We are grateful to Carolyn McKanders for teaching us about polarity management. She advises that groups must learn to distinguish between a problem to solve and a polarity to be managed. Polarities are persistent, chronic issues that are unavoidable and irresolvable. How to manage different approaches to improving student performance is a problem to solve. Balancing the need for autonomy and teamwork is a polarity to be managed. Polarities have two or more right answers that are interdependent, and they must be managed by *both/and* thinking. Both/and thinking avoids the polarization involved in beginning a thought with "but" and encourages an inclusive approach. So how can we manage both the need for autonomy and teamwork?

Polarity Management

🗆 In polarity management, groups identify the benefits of each position—autonomy and team work—then name the shortcomings of each. They seek patterns that will maximize the benefits of both while minimizing the negative aspects of either if it were done to the exclusion of the other. Readers can learn how to do this through two sources. The seminal work can be found in Barry Johnson's (1996) *Polarity Management: Identifying and Managing Unsolvable Problems.* A briefer version written by Mckanders can be found in *Unlocking Group Potential* (Garmston, 2012.)

SUMMARY

Many intractable problems seem to come from left field, yet accomplished facilitators are able to create opportunities for the group to resolve these problems. When facilitators operate at advanced levels of intervention, they usually are able to generate their intervention strategies beyond what is outlined in this book. Not only do they borrow strategies from others, but also they are skilled at combining strategies into complex heuristics, which to the novice may seem invisible. The journey begins when the beginner realizes that the facilitator is never passive, but is influencing at all times, even through being silent. As skills develop in facilitation, so do skills in communication. In the end, facilitation and intervention skills are all about communication. The accomplished facilitator is a skilled communicator.

Accomplished facilitators intervene with integrity and trust that groups move when they are ready. As Michael Grinder comments, the group is always the group's group, not the facilitator's. Skilled facilitators respond to difficult situations with purpose and flexibility. Their work is structured as journeys toward building the group's repertoire and ability to self-manage.

Facilitation is hard work. It demands 100% of presence 100% of the time. It requires consistent metacognition and emotional management. To do this, the facilitator must be in the best physical, mental, and spiritual space possible, keeping in mind that an ever-present aim is to release control as groups become better able to monitor and correct their behaviors. Yet purposeful group interaction is complex and groups will always require some form of facilitation services. The greater the emotion and the complexity of problems groups encounter, the greater need for expert facilitation.

Productive group work requires that participants commit to be open and honest, work through disagreements, and resolve conflicts. With effective facilitation, the value of working in groups improves, and groups take more and more responsibility for working effectively in all encounters, not just in meetings. The net effect is that we create a sense of renewal, hope, and reaffirm our commitment to make the world a better place. No one benefits more than our students; they deserve schools where teachers know how to work and learn together.

APPENDIX

ROOM ARRANGEMENT

The ideal meeting room is quiet, comfortable, has empty space on walls on which the group can post its work, and is free from distractions. Furniture, space, and visual displays are part of the surroundings that mediate thinking and behavior. Visual displays are more important for working groups than previously thought. Most information is received visually and when people tire, auditory processing goes first. That's one reason why room arrangement and access to visual displays is so important.

Specific tasks require conscious attention to room arrangement and the provision of materials. Each room arrangement communicates and provides structures for desired interactions. High-performing groups post charts that state outcomes for their tasks, and remind the participants of working agreements and meeting standards. These groups chart for group memory during discussions. Group memory and graphic processes support learning and retention. Charting materials such as markers, tape, pads, and sturdy flip charts are readily available. Wall space is available for charts to be posted as the group does its work.

For clarity and processing ease, we suggest that earth tones are used for text (dark green, brown, blue), black for numbering, and finally red to record votes in the decision-making meeting shown in Room Arrangement Example 1.

Room Arrangement Example 1

Figure A.1 depicts a room arrangement similar to that shown in the DVD *The Focusing Four: A Consensus Seeking Activity for Prioritizing* (Garmston & Dolcemascolo, 2009).

There are several key principles guiding this arrangement. First, participants can easily access visual data; second, they can see the facilitator, recorder, and one another; and third, because this arrangement is for a decision-making meeting, participants are seated close together with no empty chairs to prevent energy leaks.

Notice the four elements in this arrangement designed for a successful decision-making meeting.

Figure A.1   Room Arrangement 1

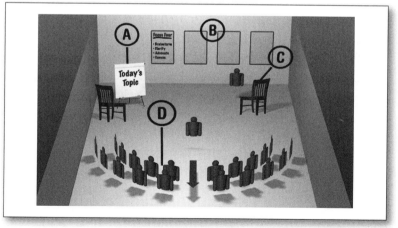

The Focusing Four: A Consensus Seeking Activity for Prioritizing © 2009 Robert Garmston and Michael Dolcemascolo. DVD Production courtesy of Media Masters, Boston, MA, www.mediamasters.biz.

A—Flip chart on which the group's task has been prerecorded.

B—Shows the placement of chart paper posted on the wall before the meeting begins. The first page displays the process the group will use, the remaining charts are blank to collect ideas during brainstorming.

C—Shows the placement for a chair, allowing the recorder to move out of the way of participant sight lines when appropriate. A second chair could be placed to the left of the room so the facilitator, too, could retire from view.

D—Shows participant seating close together with an aisle for facilitator movement.

Room Arrangement Example 2

This arrangement is designed for a small group. It shows the group, seated in a circle, with a flip chart near the facilitator.

In this design, the facilitator will both facilitate *and* record. The facilitator may choose to sit in the space near the flip chart when not visually directing the group's attention or recording.

Figure A.2   Room Arrangement 2

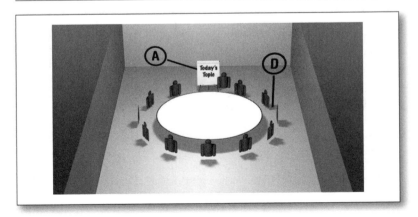

A—Shows the position for a flip chart. Because what is recorded needs to stay visual, decide before the meeting where to post pages when transitioning to write on a fresh page.

D—Shows the participant seating. Be sure to remove empty chairs from the circle. A conference table can be used in a variation of this arrangement.

The figure to the right of the chart shows the location of the facilitator. This position allows the person in this role the flexibility of standing to direct focus or charting as needed.

Room Arrangement Example 3

This arrangement shows the use of a room's corner. When working in a large space, focus can be enhanced by visually closing off room portions extraneous to the activity.

Figure A.3 Room Arrangement 3

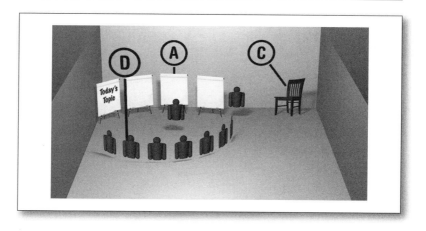

A—Shows the placement of several flip charts.

C—Indicates the placement of a chair for the facilitator or recorder.

D—Shows participant seating in a semicircle. The semicircle allows clear sight lines to the flip charts, the facilitator, and to one another.

REFERENCES

Abrams, J. (2009). *Having hard conversations.* Thousand Oaks, CA: Corwin.

Amason, A., Thompson, K., Hochwarter, W., & Harrison, A. (1995, Autumn). Conflict: An important dimension in successful management teams. *Organizational Dynamics, 24*(2), 20–35.

Bridges, W. (1980). *Transitions: Making sense of life's changes.* New York, NY: Perseus.

Chadwick, B. (2010). *Beyond conflict to consensus: An introductory learning manual.* Retrieved from http://managingwholes.com/chadwick.htm

Costa, A., & Garmston, R. (2002). *Cognitive coaching: A foundation for renaissance schools* (Rev. ed.). Lanham, MD: Roman & Littlfield.

Crum, T. (1987). *The magic of conflict: Turning a life of work into a work of art.* New York, NY: Simon & Shuster.

DeBono, E. (1985). *The six thinking hats.* New York, NY: Little, Brown & Co.

Doyle, M., & Straus, D. (1976). *How to make meetings work: The new interaction method.* New York, NY: Jove.

Duate, N. (2010). *Resonate: Present visual stories that transform audiences.* Hoboken, NJ: John Wiley & Sons.

Fullan, M. (1991). *What's worth fighting for?* Ontario, Canada: Ontario Public Schools Teachers' Federation.

Garmston, R. (1998, Spring). Graceful conflict: When you care enough use the principles of effective fighting. *Journal of Staff Development, 19*(3), 56–58.

Garmston, R. (2002, Summer). Group wise: Standards can guide success in meetings. *Journal of Staff Development, 23*(3), 74–75.

Garmston, R. (2004, Fall). Anticipate change: Design a transition meeting. *Journal of Staff Development, 25*(4), 65–66.

Garmston, R., & Dolcemascolo, M. (2009). *The focusing four: A consensus seeking activity for prioritizing: DVD viewers guide.* Highlands Ranch, CO: The Center for Adaptive Schools.

Garmston, R., & Wellman, B. (2009). *Syllabus: A sourcebook for developing collaborative groups* (5th ed.). Highlands Ranch, CO: The Center for Adaptive Schools.

Garmston, R., with von Frank, V. (2012). *Unlocking group potential to improve schools.* Thousand Oaks, CA: Corwin.

Garmston, R. (2013). *The presenter's fieldbook: A practical guide* (3rd ed.). New York, NY: Roman & Littlefield.

Garmston, R. J., & Wellman, B. (2013). *The adaptive school: A sourcebook for developing collaborative groups* (Rev. ed.). Lanham, MD: Roman & Littlefied.

Gladwell, M. (2008). *Outliers: The story of success.* New York, NY: Little, Brown & Co.

Glaser, J. (2005). *Leading through collaboration: Guiding groups to productive solutions.* Thousand Oaks, CA: Corwin.

Grinder, M. (1993). *ENVoY: Your personal guide to classroom management.* Battle Ground, WA: Michael Grinder & Associates.

Iacaboni, M. (2008). *Mirroring people: The new science about how we connect with others.* New York, NY: Farrar, Straus & Giroux.

Johnson, B. (1996). *Polarity management: Identifying and managing unsolvable problems.* Amherst, MA: HRD Press.

Kegan, R., & Lahey, L. (2009). *Immunity to change: How to overcome it and unlock the potential in yourself and your organization.* Boston, MA: Harvard Business Press.

Kendon, A. (2004). *Gesture: Visual action as utterance.* Cambridge, England.

Kieffer, G. (1988). *The strategy of meetings.* New York, NY: Simon and Schuster.

Leonard, G. (1991). *Mastery: The keys to success and long-term fulfillment.* New York, NY: Penguin.

McKay, M., Davis, M., & Fanning, P. (1983). *Messages: The communication book.* Oakland, CA: New Harbinger.

McTaggart, L. (2008). *The intention experiment: Using your thoughts to change your life and the world.* New York, NY: Simon & Schuster/ Free Press.

Michalko, M. (1991). *Thinkertoys: A handbook of business creativity for the 90's*. Berkeley, CA: Ten Speed Press.

Miller, G. A. (1956). The magical number seven, plus or minus two: Some limits on our capacity for processing information. *Psychological Review, 63*(2), 81–97.

Nisbett, R. (2003). *The geography of thought: How Asians and Westerners think differently and why*. New York, NY: Simon and Shuster.

Peck, S. (2003). *The road less traveled: A new psychology of love, traditional values and spiritual growth*. New York, NY: Touchstone.

Pew Internet. (2012). Smartphone ownership update: September 2012. Retrieved from http://www.pewinternet.org/Reports/2012/Location-based-services/Summary-of-findings/Background.aspx

Rock, D. (2009). *Your brain at work: Strategies for overcoming distraction, regaining focus and working smarter all day long*. New York, NY: Harper Business.

Scholtes, P. (1998). *The leader's handbook: A guide to inspiring your people and managing the daily workflow*. New York, NY: McGraw Hill.

Schwartz, R. M. (2002). *The skilled facilitator: Practical wisdom for developing effective groups* (2nd ed.). San Francisco, CA: Jossey-Bass.

Seamon, T. (2006, December 14). OD Blogs Abound. Message posted to blog: Here We Are. Now What? Retrieved from http://learningvoyager.blogspot.com/2006/12/od-blogs-abound.html

Sibbet, D. (2002). *Best practices for facilitation*. San Francisco, CA: Grove Consultants International.

The Sound Learning Centre. Retrieved from www.thesoundlearningcentre.co.uk/the-cause/processing/

Streibel, B. (2003). *The manager's guide to effective meetings*. New York, NY: McGraw-Hill.

Syed, M. (2010). *Bounce: Mozart, Federer, Picasso, Beckman and the science of success*. New York, NY: Harper Collins.

Weisbord, M. & Janoff, S. (2007). *Don't just do something, stand there! Ten principles for leading meetings that matter*. San Francisco, CA: Berrett-Koehler.

Zoller, K. (2010). *The choreography of presenting: The 7 essential abilities of effective presenters*. Thousand Oaks, CA: Corwin.

INDEX

Page references followed (figure) indicate an illustrated figure.

Wellman, B., 59, 74, 108
Workflow interventions
  address a refusal to follow a
    direction, 79–80
  address uneven finishes with
    group work, 81
  assist with difficulty
    transitioning, 80
  energize a quiet group, 81–82
Working agreements
  description and purpose of, 52
  evaluating, 56–57
  facilitator role in following the, 54
  going slow to go fast review of, 59
  how they function during the
    meeting, 53–54

problem locator on,
  7 (figure)
recalibrating as intervention for
  interrupters, 112
recalibrating by using a complete
  message, 54–56
reestablished as intervention for
  monopolizers, 107
regarding cell phones and texting,
  113–114
sample meeting standards and,
  52 (figure)
"suspension of judgment," 146

Zoller, K., 25, 43, 44,
  126–127

CORWIN

A SAGE Company

The Corwin logo—a raven striding across an open book—represents the union of courage and learning. Corwin is committed to improving education for all learners by publishing books and other professional development resources for those serving the field of PreK–12 education. By providing practical, hands-on materials, Corwin continues to carry out the promise of its motto: **"Helping Educators Do Their Work Better."**